THE WORD OF GOD IS WORKING:
EVERY TIME AND EVERYWHERE

THE CREATIVE POWER OF GOD'S WORD

By

PASTOR MARY I. EHICHIOYA

xulon
PRESS

Copyright © 2013 by PASTOR MARY I. EHICHIOYA

The Word Of God Is Working: Every Time And Everywhere
The Creative Power Of God's Word
by PASTOR MARY I. EHICHIOYA

Printed in the United States of America

ISBN 9781628390421

All rights reserved solely by the author. The author guarantees all contents are original and do not infringe upon the legal rights of any other person or work. No part of this book may be reproduced in any form without the permission of the author. The views expressed in this book are not necessarily those of the publisher.

Unless otherwise indicated, Bible quotations are taken from the King James Version of the Bible.

Other Versions quoted include:

New Living Translation (NLT). Copyright © 1996, 2004, 2007 by Tyndale House Foundation. Used by permission. All rights reserved.

The Message (MSG). Copyright © 1993, 1994, 1995, 1996, 2000, 2001, 2002. Used by permission of NavPress Publishing Group. Used by permission. All rights reserved.

Good News Translation (GNT). Copyright © 1992 American Bible Society. Used by permission. All rights reserved.

English Standard Version (ESV). Copyright © 2001 by Crossway, a publishing ministry of Good News Publishers. Used by permission. All rights reserved.

New English Translation (NET Bible). Copyright ©1996-2006 by Biblical Studies Press, L.L.C. Used by permission. All rights reserved.

Amplified Bible (AMP). Copyright © 1954, 1958, 1962, 1964, 1965, 1987 by The Lockman Foundation. Used by permission. All rights reserved.

YOU VERSION FREE BIBLE APP. © 2013 Yahoo!

www.xulonpress.com

TABLE OF CONTENTS

FORWARD vii
DEDICATION ix
ACKNOWLEDGEMENT xi
PREFACE xiii
INTRODUCTION xvii

CHAPTER ONE 23
CHAPTER TWO 35
CHAPTER THREE 45
CHAPTER FOUR 54

CONCLUSION 63
WHAT TO DO 65
DAILY FAITH DECLARATIONS 69

FORWARD

This book focuses on the need for believers to turn to God's Word for guidance in situations and challenges in their lives, allowing scripture to strengthen their belief in God's power to change all areas of their lives. Readers will be encouraged to speak out loud God's Word in any situation and will feel the peace in knowing God's power is changing their situation as they speak.

- The author's passion for God's Word is evident throughout the book, intensified by her knowledge of scripture that helps to amplify her points to the readers. Having also stories of God's work happening in the author's life will support her claims of how God's Word can change any situation for the better.

- Having scripture in bold and italic lettering will allow the scripture to draw the attention of readers while reading and can be a helpful resource to look back on as the reader continues reading the book.

- The faith declarations at the end of the book will be beneficial to both new and seasoned believers in Jesus Christ as it encourages them to become more open and cognizant about their faith each day.

Blair Townley
Editor
Xulon Press, a part of Salem Communications

DEDICATION

This book is lovingly dedicated to the ever living memory of my husband, Pastor Samuel Idahoise Ehichioya who was my beloved friend, brother, coach, pastor, lover, daddy and husband. O Boy, my joy is that you are rejoicing in the bosom of the Lord in glory and that our separation is only temporary.

ACKNOWLEDGEMENT

I am eternally grateful to my Heavenly Father who gave His Son, my Lord Jesus Christ to be my Substitute. He took my place of sin, rejection and condemnation and He qualified me to become God's own righteousness in Him.

I was judged and punished in Him. He purchased me with His blood and He gave me to God the Father as His inheritance. Now, I am free to live for the Living God in righteousness through His Spirit who lives in me. I am now accepted in Him and God has put His very life and Spirit in my spirit. I now belong to the class of God and I am justified and seated with Christ in the place of power; at the right hand of God the Father in the heavenly places.

I thank You Father, Son and Holy Spirit for Your wisdom, love, and grace that made this book a reality. I am born for the glorious life in Christ and it can only get better for me. The same is true of every genuine believer in Christ Jesus. Hallelujah!

I am also deeply appreciative of all the people God has used and that He is still using to teach me His Word. My special thanks go to the members of the Central Executive Council of the Believers Loveworld Nation, a.k.a. Christ Embassy, under the presidency of my dearly beloved Pastor Chris Oyakhilome; who are teaching me the Word of God through His Spirit. I thank you Pastors for teaching me the Word of God. I love you all.

I want to also thank Dr Mary O of To His Glory Publishing Company Inc. USA, for an excellent job of formatting and editing, at a minimal price. God bless you.

PREFACE

The Word of God is working every time and everywhere; producing results, because the Holy Spirit who works through God's Word is everywhere at the same time. God speaks and His Spirit brings it to pass. He is the same Spirit that raised Jesus Christ from the dead. We were raised with Him and were justified by His resurrection. That same Spirit lives in us who are true believers today. Just as He manifests God's Words, He also brings our faith proclamations to pass. The spiritual truth is that the Word of God and the words that we speak have creative powers because they are supernatural. What the Word did in ancient times that are recorded in the Bible, it is still doing today.

> *"In the beginning was the Word, and the Word was with God, and the Word was God. The same was in the beginning with God. All things were made by him; and without him was not anything made that was made. In him was life; and the life was the light of men. And the light shineth in darkness; and the darkness comprehended it not"* John 1:1-5.

This book is written to share with you the power of some of the great truths in the Word of God that I have been favored and privileged by God to have been taught over the years. I have come to know by teaching and by experience what God's Word in the hearts and mouths of true believers can create for us. I have also come to know that whatsoever we believe God for, or declare, and or act upon, we surely get.

It is true that words are the most powerful things in the universe; especially when it is the Word of God in the mouth of a believer in Christ Jesus. The LORD God said the following in **Joshua 1:8:**

> *"This book of the law shall not depart out of thy mouth; but thou shall meditate therein day and night, that thou mayest observe to do according to all that is written therein: for then thou shall have good success."*

The Word of God is God's Instructional Manual for our lives on earth. It is His recipe for good success. It is the Manual that tells us who we are, where we came from and where we are going. It tells us our reason for being here on earth and what we are assigned by God to do here. God's Instructional Manual gives us the reason we were born into this world. In other words, it gives our lives purpose and meaning; it gives us our reason for living. It is God's gift to us and it is our agent for absolute change for a better life. God's Word is His tool for making us to become all He designed us to be. In God's estimation of man, living without this Manual means living an empty life. What this means is that you can make your life wonderful by following God's Instructional Manual for your life. The choice is ours since God made us to be free moral agents (gave us a free will). **We have been students in various schools and we have taken tests and we know that if a student does not read the examiner's instructions before answering the test questions, the probability of passing that test is zero. It is the same way when it comes to God's Instructional Manual, we cannot pass life examinations without following the instructions of the Author of life.**

Christianity is not a religion but the life of God in a man's spirit and it is this life that makes the believer a supernatural man or woman. It requires faith in God's Word and a corresponding confession of that faith. Therefore, Christianity is called the great confession. **Many Christians who are defeated in life are defeated because they believe and say the wrong things. They talk the problem instead**

of the solution. The Word of God in our mouths is the solution to any challenge we may face in this life. The spiritual truth is that wrong speaking (confession) empowers the enemy as we read in **Proverbs 18:20-21:**

> *"A man's belly shall be satisfied with the fruit of his mouth; and with the increase of his lips shall he be filled. Death and life are in the power of the tongue: and they that love it shall eat the fruit thereof."*
>
> **James 3:2** and **6** tell us, *"For in many things we offend all. If any man offend not in word, the same is a perfect man, and able also to bridle the whole body... And the tongue is a fire, a world of iniquity: so is the tongue amongst our members, that it defileth the whole body, and setteth on fire the course of nature; and it is set on fire of hell."*

Right beliefs and right confessions that are faith filled put us over in life (gives us victory) but the words which we speak that do not align with God's Word only lead to defeat in life. As believers, our right confessions make all things possible for us as the Lord informed us in **Mark 9:23:**

> *"Jesus said unto him, If thou canst believe, all things are possible to him that believeth."*

The spiritual law is that when we believe and then speak that belief in faith, we have what we say. In other words, what we say is what comes to us.

It grieves my heart whenever I see or hear people constantly confessing the situations and circumstances that they are dealing with instead of confessing their faith in the power of God's Word. It grieves me because I know that they do not know any better than to confess their problems. There is so much struggling as a result of this ignorance. God called us to a life of grace, power, and glory; not to a life of struggles and stress. We can effect changes in our unpalatable situations by agreeing with God and His Word, and saying what God has said instead of what the situation is saying. **My desire to help others know what God has honored me to know concerning the spiritual truth of these things by His Spirit gave birth to this book.** I know there are more detailed materials out there on the same subject but this is my own contribution by His grace. The Spirit of God said the following through Paul in **2 Timothy 2:2:**

> *"And the things that thou hast heard of me among many witnesses, the same commit thou to faithful men, who shall be able to teach others also."*

This is my main reason for writing this book: I was taught some vital truths which are helping me to live the victorious life in Christ Jesus today and I am sharing these truths with you in this book. I expect you to learn these truths from this book and I pray that you will be in a position to teach others what you have been taught by reading it and it is working for you.

INTRODUCTION

*I*n the preface, I stated that **the Word of God is working every time and everywhere; producing results.** This is because the Spirit of God who works the Word is everywhere at the same time. I would like you to take a look at this excerpt below in order to gain an understanding of **who the Word really is**:

"Some say I am just an expression of an idea and that I have no real effect on people's lives. Some don't believe in me at all. **I wish they knew me better**. I have been misused, misspoken, misinterpreted, and misunderstood; yet I remain faithful and true. **The Word of God is faithful and true.** I am far more than mere words. **I am Spirit and I am Life**. I was there in the beginning. When I spoke, things were created and everything in the universe is upheld by me. I am quick and powerful and I am sharper than any two-edged sword. I am the spirit of faith and I am truth. **I am a light unto your path and a lamp unto your feet if you choose to follow me**.

I am incorruptible seed and **when I am spoken in faith God, watch over me to make sure I perform. I do not return void or incomplete but I accomplish that which I was sent to do**. I am very pure, unchanging and holy. I am forever settled in heaven. I am steadfast and **I am at work all the time. I can be trusted and I am never wrong.** I am the sword of the Spirit and I am like a hammer; yet I can wash your soul like the purest of water. **When I am spoken things are established in your life. I am eternal. I am sweeter than honey on your lips. When I enter your heart, I give light and understanding. If you love me you will have great peace and nothing shall offend you. I give you wisdom and I am life to those who find me and health to all their flesh.**

If you love me and keep me in your heart, when you go out, I will lead you. When you sleep, I will keep you and when you awake, I will talk with you. When you need instruction, I am there to instruct you and when you need correction, I am there to correct you. I know I can change your life. I am just waiting to be loved, spoken, and believed in. I have every answer to every question that you will ever have. If you would meditate on me day and night, keep me before your eyes and in your mouth, you will make your way prosperous and you will have good success. If I were in your heart in abundance, you would be speaking me all the time. I AM God's Word."

According to **Romans 8:38-39**, as believers in Christ Jesus, we have become inseparably one with God.

> *"For I am persuaded, that neither death, nor life, nor angels, nor principalities, nor powers, nor things present, nor things to come, Nor height, nor depth, nor any other creature, shall be able to separate us from the love of God, which is in Christ Jesus our Lord."*

When we speak God's Word, it is God talking through us and it must happen just as we spoke. **God is a faith God; meaning that God operates in faith and He requires faith.** We are His "faith children" and therefore, must cooperate with Him. The words we speak are powerful demonstrations of our faith.

INTRODUCTION

I also want to share with you what I learned about how God operates that I think we should all imitate. It is found in **1 Corinthians 1:26-28**:

> *"26For you see your calling, brethren, that not many wise according to the flesh, not many mighty, not many noble, are called. 27 But God has chosen the foolish things of the world to put to shame the wise, and God has chosen the weak things of the world to put to shame the things which are mighty; 28 and the base things of the world and the things which are despised God has chosen, and the things which are not, to bring to nothing the things that are."*

Do you see the pattern here? God's chosen way of doing things is directly opposite of what we think is natural. That being said, we can see why this faith principle is so misunderstood. You must force yourself to think this way and trust that God knows what He is talking about in His Word and in your life. Keep in mind verse 27. God has chosen the foolish and weak things to put to shame the "wise and mighty"...and here we are ...**The Chosen!**

That thought alone should produce a little humility. God chose this method of using things that are not manifested in this earth realm (things that you cannot see, smell, touch, etc.) to bring to NOTHING the things that ARE manifested. This is what we see in the New Testament healings by Jesus Christ during His earthly ministry. Practically, to every miracle of healing, He added a comment such as, *"Thy faith hath saved thee...;"* *"According to your faith be it done unto you...;"* *"Thy faith hath made thee whole...;"* *"If you can believe, all things are possible to him that believes,"* etc. God has chosen the unseen; the force of faith (the thing that is NOT manifest) to bring to nothing the things that are made manifest such as sickness, disease, poverty, oppression, etc.

One great enemy of our faith is <u>fear</u> of the visible and the tangible. The Church has become slave to the visible and the tangible. This principle of <u>*"Calling things that are not as though they were"*</u> <u>is very vital to our walk in this physical realm.</u> As I said earlier, we must also understand the power of the words that we speak. Therefore, I think that **John 1: 1-3** holds a vital key for us:

> *"¹In the beginning was the Word and the Word was with God, and the Word was God. ² He was in the beginning with God. ³All things were made through Him and without Him nothing was made that was made."*

We must realize that God has not changed. He now indwells the regenerate man (a born again Christian) and still works by this one unchangeable process of faith:

- **The Father thinks His thoughts.**
- **The Son speaks His creative word by faith.**
- **The Spirit manifests the substance in the natural realm.**
- **One responsibility lies with man and it is so pivotal that ALL the outcome is dependent on this one activity — man must carry out the process of faith.**

This is not a magic formula or a magician's trick. This is NOT trying to "get God to do something." This is simply **man co-operating** with God on the inside and yielding to this creative/re-creative process. **The thought of faith which is expressed by the word of faith, results in the substance of faith.** We must embrace the power of the unseen realm; God's realm where true power comes from — things you cannot see. Here is the principle:

> **Romans 4:17**: *"(as it is written, "I have made you a father of many nations") in the presence of Him whom he believed—God, who gives life to the dead and calls those things which do not exist as though they did."*

God uses Abraham (the father of our faith) as the example for this process of faith. God changed his name from ABRAM to ABRAHAM. Abraham literally means "father of a multitudes." Was he a father of a multitude when his name was changed? No, **but when God called**

INTRODUCTION

him Abraham, the force of faith was released and the Spirit of God had a legal right to bring it to pass in the natural realm for Abraham. This is the "Mechanics of Faith" in action.

Concerning the "Mechanics of Faith," let us look at an example in the Lord Jesus' life and ministry by examining the following scriptures:

> **Mark 11:12-14**: *"¹²And on the morrow, when they were come from Bethany, he was hungry: ¹³And seeing a fig tree afar off having leaves, he came, if haply he might find anything thereon: and when he came to it, he found nothing but leaves; for the time of figs was not yet. ¹⁴And Jesus answered and said unto it, No man eat fruit of thee hereafter forever. And his disciples heard it."*

> **Mark 11:20-22**: *"²⁰And in the morning, as they passed by, they saw the fig tree dried up from the roots. ²¹And Peter calling to remembrance saith unto him, Master, behold, the fig tree which thou cursedst is withered away. ²²And Jesus answering saith unto them, Have faith in God."*

Even Jesus, when He spoke to the fig tree did not see results that very minute. In other words, His disciples did not see the results of His "cursing the fig tree" until the next morning. Many people get discouraged when they confess God's Word and do not see results right away. Meaning that, some people speak God's Word to their disease or problem; they truly declare what God's Word says about their situation and if it does not manifest when they think it should, they give up and cast away their confidence. They do not hold fast to their confession so they get no results. **Perseverance is the key to getting results with God.** This is why we are given the following admonition in **Hebrews 10:23**:

> *"Let us hold fast the profession of our faith without wavering; (for he is faithful that promised."*

The word "profession" is the same word used for confession. We must trust God that what He said is true and we must trust the "process of faith" that He has established —**calling those things that are not manifest as though they were.** Also, we are told in **1 John 5:4** that our faith overcomes the world:

> "... *And this is the victory that overcometh the world, even our faith.*"

Prayer: Our dear heavenly Father, we thank You and rejoice at Your Word as the people who have found great treasure. Your Word is our life, and has the final authority over us, and all that we do. We will forever yield ourselves to the Lordship of Your Word to mold, correct, and fashion us into the glorious personalities that You have ordained us to be, in Jesus' Name. Amen.

Confession: Precious Father, we thank and worship You, for fully dressing and equipping us for life with Your Word. We are strengthened, fortified, and energized for victory through the power of Your Word and the might of Your Spirit. We maintain our victory and dominion over Satan and the forces of darkness today, and with our divine armory, we extinguish all the fiery darts of the wicked, in the Name of our Lord Jesus Christ. Amen.

Endnote: "Used by permission from truthpressure.com"

Chapter One

WHAT WE SAY IS WHAT WE GET

Dearly beloved of God, our Lord Jesus said in **Mark 11:23** that **we will have whatsoever we say.** Meaning that our words will create for us what we say. He did not qualify it. Whether we meant it or not is not the issue because our words are powerful. **Romans 10:10** tells us that, *"For with the heart man believeth unto righteousness; and with the mouth confession is made unto salvation."* This is how powerful the words we speak are. Speaking forth what we believe about our salvation in Christ Jesus, catapults us into salvation, into a life of victory, into success, into prosperity and into divine health. We do not stop there. **To continue to enjoy this wonderful package of salvation in Christ, we have to learn to agree with God's Word and to continually use our mouths to give life to the blessings in the package.** We can use our mouths to keep our bodies healthy by continually speaking forth words that are consistent with the Word of God. What we said yesterday determined our today. Therefore, what we are saying today will determine our tomorrow; it is a spiritual law.

This is why the Lord Jesus said in **Mark 11:23:**

> *"For verily I __say__ unto you, That whosoever shall __say__ unto this mountain, Be thou removed, and be thou cast into the sea; and shall not doubt in his heart, but*

*shall believe that those things which he **saith** shall come to pass; he shall have whatsoever he **saith.**"*

When you look at this scripture closely, you will find out that the Lord mentioned *"shall believe"* only once. The word *say or saith* was mentioned four times. **This goes to show that the saying part of our salvation after we've believed is very vital to our doing well or living the victorious Christian life we have been born into**. As believers in Christ, we can talk ourselves out of any situation or circumstance by saying or confessing the Word of God concerning that situation or circumstance. For instance, when you notice a growth or a swelling in any part of your body, your first reaction as a believer should not be to give it a name or to run off to find out what it is. You do not know what it is; God knows and has already dealt with it in His Son on your behalf.

Therefore, the growth or swelling you are seeing is a **mirage**. It is a lying vanity. Go to the Word and find out what God said about your health in Christ? Hear Him in **Isaiah 53:4-5**:

"Surely he hath borne our griefs, and carried our sorrows: yet we did esteem him stricken, smitten of God, and afflicted. But he was wounded for our transgressions; he was bruised for our iniquities: the chastisement of our peace was upon him; and with his stripes we are healed."

Hear Him again in **1 Peter 2:24**:

*"Who his own self bare our sins in his own body on the tree that we, being dead to sins, should live unto righteousness: by whose stripes ye **were** healed."*

Stand on what God has said concerning you and keep saying it because when you continue to say it, you will have what you say. I remember when I had a growth in my body and I told my husband about it. His reaction was, "Why are you talking about it? Don't you know what to do? Talk to it and kill it!" As a result, I stood on the above scriptures and kept declaring every day that "if I was **healed** then, I am healed now. What is dead does not grow. Therefore, growth, I command you to die from your roots and dematerialize; get out of my body and never to return in Jesus' Name." **I did not go to see any doctor but I kept declaring the Word and as a result, I had what I said.** As the Lord said I would; glory to His Name! There is great power in our words so, learn to speak what God has said concerning you in His Word. The Word is written for our edification.

Everything you require for a victorious and glorious life is already in you as a believer in Christ. You activate them by speaking them forth. You can change what you do not like in your life with the Word of God in your heart and in your mouth. Say what God has said about us and set yourself in agreement with Him. Declare, repeat, and confess what He has said in His Word concerning us. This will set you on the course of fulfilling your divine destiny on this earth and of reaching your potentials in Christ.

God releases His power through His Word. When He speaks, the Holy Spirit goes into action. We release our faith through what we say. When we speak what God has said concerning us, the Holy Spirit goes into action. Everything we believe enough to speak out comes to pass; be it positive or negative. We have to understand the power of words. Negative words should not be spoken by us as believers. Therefore, we have to watch what we say. We have to give God the control of our hearts and tongues by knowing Him through His Word and agreeing with Him. It is therefore imperative that we cooperate with and allow the Holy Spirit to help us by educating our spirits (the real us) with the Word of God. When the Holy Spirit is in control in our lives, we become wise with the wisdom of God.

We can reframe our worlds by the words we speak because of our spiritual education. This is what God wants to give us; His Word in our spirits. It will create in us and for us what it talks about. It will make us what it talks about. It will give us our hearts' desires because it has the intrinsic power to transform our lives and circumstances. The power is in the spoken Word. There is inherent power in the Word of God and this power is released by speaking forth the Word. We have to form the good habit of speaking God's Word out loud daily. The Kingdom principle is to call those things that are not as if they were, through the power of the Holy Spirit in us.

This faith action on our part gives the Spirit of God the legal right to bring to pass for us in the natural, what we are declaring. Then we will live the glorious and victorious lives that God gave His Son for us to live and to enjoy on earth and ever after. According to **John 10:10**, the Lord Jesus came to give us life and *"life more abundantly"* (life to be lived to the fullness). **What this means is that He is not about to do it because He has done it and has given us all things to enjoy.** He has already suffered on our behalf and His vicarious suffering has ushered us into the glory-life. Let us understand and live the life of glory that should follow the sufferings of Christ. He has abolished death, disease and failure. He brought us into a life of glory, honor, dignity, and excellence. God's power is in His Word.

True meaning and enjoyment in life are found only in God and in His Word. Real life comes from God living inside us and our joy comes from reflecting the light of His presence. Think on these scriptures below:

John 14:6-7:

> *"Jesus saith unto him, I am the way, the truth, and the life: no man cometh unto the Father, but by me. If ye had known me, ye should have known my Father also: and from henceforth ye know him, and have seen him."*

Revelation 21:5-7:

> *"And he that sat upon the throne said, Behold, I make all things new. And he said unto me, Write: for these words are true and faithful. And he said unto me, It is done. I am Alpha and Omega, the beginning and the end. I will give unto him that is athirst of the fountain of the water of life freely. He that overcometh shall*

inherit all things; and I will be his God, and he shall be my son."

Outside of God and His Word, life is empty and without meaning; no matter how seemingly successful and enjoyable it may appear here and now to the natural man who has no relationship with God as Father through Christ. Think about what these scriptures below are saying:

Mark 8:34-38:

> *"And when he had called the people unto him with his disciples also, he said unto them, whosoever will come after me, let him deny himself, and take up his cross, and follow me. For whosoever will save his life shall lose it; but whosoever shall lose his life for my sake and the gospel's, the same shall save it. For what shall it profit a man, if he shall gain the whole world, and lose his own soul? Or what shall a man give in exchange for his soul? Whosoever therefore shall be ashamed of me and of my words in this adulterous and sinful generation; of him also shall the Son of man be ashamed, when he cometh in the glory of his Father with the holy angels."*

Revelation 21:8:

> *"But the fearful, and unbelieving, and the abominable, and murderers, and whoremongers, and sorcerers, and idolaters, and all liars, shall have their part in the lake which burneth with fire and brimstone: which is the second death."*

2 Thessalonians 2:10-13:

> *"And with all deceivableness of unrighteousness in them that perish because they received not the love*

of the truth, that they might be saved. And for this cause God shall send them strong delusion, that they should believe a lie: That they all might be damned who believed not the truth, but had pleasure in unrighteousness. But we are bound to give thanks always to God for you, brethren beloved of the Lord, because God hath from the beginning chosen you to salvation through sanctification of the Spirit and belief of the truth."

What a life that awaits the unbelieving and the carnal Christian? God's Word in the Bible is God's Instructional Manual for our lives as true believers in Christ Jesus. This is the only way that God's Spirit can help us to know God. It is also the only way that we can know who we are in Christ, what belongs to us in Him and what we can do. Sadly, many professing believers are too busy with other things to read, study, or meditate on the Word of God in the Bible. We all need to give the Word of God the preeminence in our lives and allow the grace of God to take us where He wants us to be. God has a blueprint on everyone on earth and His Word will make us all He has designed us to be.

The Lord Jesus said in **Matthew 6:33**, *"But seek ye first the kingdom of God, and his righteousness; and all these things shall be added unto you."* Therefore, let us put God first and let us trust Him to be who He says He is and to do in and through us, what He says He can do and has done for us in Christ.

As a result of the finished work of the Lord Jesus Christ, true believers in Him have vitally become the righteousness of God. This is why the scriptures say 2 **Corinthians 5:21**, *"For he hath made him to be sin for us, who knew no sin; that we might be made the righteousness of God in him"* The Lord Jesus made it possible for God to justly forgive us sinners and to still remain a just God:

"Whom God hath set forth to be a propitiation through faith in his blood, to declare his righteousness for the remission of sins that are past, through the forbearance of God; To declare, I say, at this time his

righteousness: that he might be just, and the justifier of him which believeth in Jesus" (Romans 3:25-26).

In Christ Jesus, God gave us His kind of life and His nature of righteousness. This is the good news! That God's love is not like human love because Christ died not for His friends but for His enemies. It was while we were yet sinners that He died for us. The argument is: if while we were yet sinners, God loved us so much that Christ died for us, how much more now shall we having been justified (freed from sin) by His blood, be saved from the displeasure of God. All these things happened because He died for us. The main point is that "Christ died for us." By His finished work, He qualified us to be accepted into God's family.

By His blood, He purchased us and gave us to God the Father as gifts — *"And they sung a new song, saying, Thou art worthy to take the book, and to open the seals thereof: for thou wast slain, and hast redeemed us to God by thy blood out of every kindred, and tongue, and people, and nation; And hast made us unto our God kings and priests: and we shall reign on the earth"* —**Revelations 5:9-10**. We are now in the class of God because of His grace wherein we stand. We have become one with Him and we are His very own children. All praise to God the Father of our Lord Jesus Christ! It is by His great mercy and grace that we have been born again because God raised Jesus Christ from the dead for us. Now, we live with great expectation and we have a priceless inheritance that is kept in heaven for us. It is pure and undefiled; beyond the reach of change and decay. Take a close look at some of the things that God has done for us in Christ that are outlined in the following scriptures:

Ephesians 2:6:

> *"And hath <u>raised us up together</u>, and <u>made us sit together in heavenly places in Christ Jesus</u>."*

Colossians 1:12-14:

> "Giving thanks unto the Father, which hath <u>made us meet to be partakers of the inheritance of the saints in light</u>: Who hath <u>delivered us from the power of darkness</u>, and <u>hath translated us into the kingdom of his dear Son</u>: In whom <u>we have redemption through his blood, even the forgiveness of sins</u>."

1 John 4:17:

> "Herein is our love made perfect, that we may <u>have boldness in the Day of Judgment</u>: **because as he is, so are we in this world**."

1 Peter 1:3-5:

> "Blessed be the God and Father of our Lord Jesus Christ, which according to his abundant mercy hath begotten us again unto a lively hope by the resurrection of Jesus Christ from the dead, To an inheritance incorruptible, and undefiled, and that fadeth not away, reserved in heaven for you, Who are kept by the power of God through faith unto salvation ready to be revealed in the last time."

What a glorious life we have in Christ! What joy to know that God is in us and we are in Him! The Apostle Paul wrote about this in **Colossians 1:27-28**:

> "To whom God would make known what is the riches of the glory of this mystery among the Gentiles; which is Christ in you, the hope of glory: Whom we preach, warning every man, and teaching every man in all wisdom; that we may present every man perfect in Christ Jesus."

And also in **Colossians 3:3**:

> *"For ye are dead, and your life is hid with Christ in God."*

The Apostle John also wrote the following in **1 John 4:4**:

> *"Ye are of God, little children, and have overcome them: because greater is he that is in you, than he that is in the world."*

You see, we can now live for Christ, expressing His glory, power, righteousness, life, and character, through the Greater One that lives in us. Therefore, when we speak, it is God talking and it must happen as we have spoken it. It cannot come back unaccomplished. It must prosper in that, which it has been sent. The Prophet Isaiah also wrote this in **Isaiah 55:10-11**:

> *"For as the rain cometh down, and the snow from heaven, and returneth not thither, but watereth the earth, and maketh it bring forth and bud, that it may give seed to the sower, and bread to the eater: So shall my word be that goeth forth out of my mouth: it shall not return unto me void, but it shall accomplish that which I please, and it shall prosper in the thing whereto I sent it."*

Hebrews 13:5-6:

> *"Let your conversation be without covetousness; and be content with such things as ye have: for he hath said, I will never leave thee, nor forsake thee. So that we may boldly say, The Lord is my helper, and I will not fear what man shall do unto me."*

Therefore, our responsibility is to apply the spiritual thus: **He has said, that we may boldly say (repeat and declare) what He has said.** Our words produce fruits or results. Why? This is because, through the Gospel of our Lord Jesus Christ, we have obtained peace with God. Whereas as sinners we were enemies of God; rebels under His divine displeasure, but now, we have turned to Him and are reconciled to Him and we have obtained forgiveness through faith. God is not reconciled to us but as genuine believers, we are to Him. His love ever shines and is shown in His Gospel. He has pardoned and received us in Christ because we have ceased from our rebellion and have turned to Him. Therefore, in His mercy and grace, we are now one with Him.

We can now boldly say what He said concerning us and get results in our lives and circumstances. We can create what we want by God's faith which He dealt to us at our new birth and through the Holy Spirit who lives in us. As stated in **Romans 12:3**, it is according to His plan for us:

> *"For I say, through the grace given unto me, to every man that is among you, not to think of himself more highly than he ought to think; but to think soberly, according as God hath dealt to every man the measure of faith."*

Also, **Galatians 2:20** explains to us that **we function by the faith of our Lord Jesus Chris. His faith never fails:**

> *"I am crucified with Christ: nevertheless I live; yet not I, but Christ liveth in me: and **the life which I now live in the flesh I live by the faith of the Son of God, who loved me, and gave himself for me**."*

Beloved, for our all-round supernatural prosperity, abundance, and success, here now and hereafter, let us meditate on these things; give ourselves entirely to them that our progress may be evident to all — 1 Timothy 4:15. It is important that we know with revelation that just because God has planned something does not mean it will happen on earth. He expects us to make it happen. God is not a man. Right from creation, God gave the earth to the children of men to run. In other words, He gave man dominion over the earth — He said in **Genesis 1:26**, *"...And let them have dominion over...and over all the earth."* God created the earth and manifests Himself in it but He does not belong to it. He is beyond the earth but God needs man's cooperation to function on the earth because He does not violate His Word that man should be the one to have dominion over the earth. This is why we must speak God's Word in consent to His plan and when we do, we give the Holy Spirit the legal right to bring it to pass in our lives. Everything God created He spoke into being.

We are made in His image and likeness. In other words, we are made to look like Him and to function like Him. The earth is man's domain. Everything God has ever done on earth, He did through men; read your Bible. What God does is to show us His plan or will. Therefore, we have to know His will, find out His principles and know how His Kingdom functions from His Word. Then, by meditating (speaking and acting) on what we find out, we sow the right seeds. We should water these seeds with our faith confessions thereby, making God's will come to pass in our lives through His Spirit that lives in every true believer in Christ Jesus. It is our duty to put the Word of God to work on earth. Jesus has given us the victory. Therefore, we have to live that victorious life here and now on earth. There is nothing to be victorious over in heaven. It is celebration galore there.

Pray this prayer: My dear heavenly Father, I thank You for making me in Your own image and likeness, to look like You and to function as You do. I am grateful Lord that You affectionately care for me, and that You lovingly watch over me, showing Yourself strong on my behalf all the time. You are very personal with me, and You rejoice over me with singing. You know me by name; and You are concerned with everything that has to do with me. There is no detail of my life here on earth that is too insignificant for You to get involve in. Your delight is for me to live joyfully in peace, prosperity and righteousness every day. Lover and Bishop of my soul, my Father forever, my focus is on You alone, and I trust You with all my heart and life. You are my Nourisher, Sustainer, and bread- Provider; my trust and hope are in You; therefore, I am confident of a glorious today, and a rewarding tomorrow, knowing that Your perfect will shall be accomplished in me, in the Name of Jesus, my Lord. Amen.

CHAPTER TWO

IT IS OUR JOB TO MAKE GOD'S WILL COME TO PASS

The Bible contains the Word of God. It is to be studied, believed, meditated on, and lived. **We have the responsibility to make God's will come to pass in our lives and in our world.** How do we do this? **As imitators of God!** The Holy Spirit told us to imitate God in all that we do as His dear children — *"Be ye therefore imitators of God, as beloved Children"* (Ephesians 5:1 ASV).

God is a faith God and as believers in Him, we are His faith children. He spoke the universe into existence. For example, He conceived what He wanted the earth to be like at creation. He had the picture in His Spirit of what He wanted the chaotic earth to be like and as He spoke, it came into being. Let us take a look at the scriptures so that we can understand how God creates by saying or speaking forth His Word. As we have read in the Bible, apart from man, God spoke everything else that He created into existence but He made us in His image and likeness. We have His creative abilities in us to make His will to come to pass in our lives and in our world. It is our job to do this in order to bring glory to God and to bring blessings to men.

We are the sons and daughters of God that the world is waiting for to manifest the glory of God. This is why "Religious Christianity" will not win the world to Christ Jesus because the world needs to see Jesus in action in our lives and through us. The world is tired of religion so we have to reveal Jesus and demonstrate His power through the Holy Spirit to the world. The Lord Jesus bought the **whole field**; every soul on earth belongs to Him. In **Matthew 13:38; 44**, we learn that the world is the field:

> *"Again, the kingdom of heaven is like unto treasure hid in a field; the which when a man hath found, he hideth, and for joy thereof goeth and selleth all that he hath, and buyeth that field ...The field is the world."*

The Holy Spirit shows us how much God loves us in **John 3:15-19**:

> *"That whosoever believeth in him should not perish, but have eternal life. For God so loved the world, that he gave his only begotten Son, that whosoever believeth in him should not perish, but have everlasting life. For God sent not his Son into the world to condemn the world; but that the world through him might be saved. He that believeth on him is not condemned: but he that believeth not is condemned already, because he hath not believed in the name of the only begotten Son of God. And this is the condemnation, that light is come into the world, and men loved darkness rather than light, because their deeds were evil."*

Jesus gave His all to purchase us from eternal damnation. Therefore, we must give our all to receive all He did for us. He has equipped us for the job. Now, let us see God at creation because we were designed to be like Him and to function like Him because according to **1 John 4:17**, we are as He is in this world —*"Herein is our love made perfect, that we may have boldness in the Day of Judgment: because as he is, so are we in this world."* **Genesis 1:1-31** shows us God creative power and faith:

> *"In the beginning God created the heaven and the earth. And the earth was without form, and void;*

and darkness was upon the face of the deep. And the Spirit of God moved upon the face of the waters. **And God said,** *Let there be light: and there was light. And God saw the light, that it was good: and God divided the light from the darkness. And God called the light Day, and the darkness he called Night. And the evening and the morning were the first day.*

And God said, *Let there be a firmament in the midst of the waters, and let it divide the waters from the waters. And God made the firmament, and divided the waters which were under the firmament from the waters which were above the firmament: and it was so. And God called the firmament Heaven. And the evening and the morning were the second day.*

And God said, *Let the waters under the heaven be gathered together unto one place, and let the dry land appear: and it was so. And God called the dry land Earth; and the gathering together of the waters called he Seas: and God saw that it was good.*

And God said, *Let the earth bring forth grass, the herb yielding seed, and the fruit tree yielding fruit after his kind, whose seed is in itself, upon the earth: and it was so. And the earth brought forth grass, and herb yielding seed after his kind, and the tree yielding fruit, whose seed was in itself, after his kind: and God saw that it was good. And the evening and the morning were the third day.*

And God said, *Let there be lights in the firmament of the heaven to divide the day from the night; and let them be for signs, and for seasons, and for days, and years: And let them be for lights in the firmament of the heaven to give light upon the earth: and it was so. And God made two great lights; the greater light* to rule the day, and the lesser light to rule the night: he made the stars also. And God set them in the firmament of the heaven to give light upon the earth, and to rule over the day and over the night, and to divide the light from the darkness: and God saw that it was good. And the evening and the morning were the fourth day.

<u>And God said,</u> Let the waters bring forth abundantly the moving creature that hath life, and fowl that may fly above the earth in the open firmament of heaven. And God created great whales, and every living creature that moveth, which the waters brought forth abundantly, after their kind, and every winged fowl after his kind: and God saw that it was good. And God blessed them, saying, Be fruitful, and multiply, and fill the waters in the seas, and let fowl multiply in the earth. And the evening and the morning were the fifth day. And God said, Let the earth bring forth the living creature after his kind, cattle, and creeping thing, and beast of the earth after his kind: and it was so. And God made the beast of the earth after his kind, and cattle after their kind, and everything that creepeth upon the earth after his kind: and God saw that it was good.

<u>And God said:</u> Let us make man in our image, after our likeness: and let them have dominion over the fish of the sea, and over the fowl of the air, and over the cattle, and over all the earth, and over every creeping thing that creepeth upon the earth.

<u>So God created man in his own image, in the image of God created he him; male and female created he them. And God blessed them, and God said unto them, Be fruitful, and multiply, and replenish the earth, and subdue it: and have dominion over the</u>

<u>fish of the sea, and over the fowl of the air, and over every living thing that moveth upon the earth</u>. And God said, Behold, I have given you every herb bearing seed, which is upon the face of all the earth, and every tree, in the which is the fruit of a tree yielding seed; to you it shall be for meat. And to every beast of the earth, and to every fowl of the air, and to everything that creepeth upon the earth, wherein there is life, I have given every green herb for meat: and it was so. And God saw everything that he had made, and, behold, it was very good. And the evening and the morning were the sixth day."

We can only imitate God by meditating on what He said concerning us in His Word and this is very necessary and powerful. God gave us the ability to speak like Him. Therefore, we can declare Rhema or the spoken and creative Word of God as He said in **Job 22:28** –"Thou *shalt also decree a thing, and it shall be established unto thee: and the light shall shine upon thy ways*." **He also gave us imaginative ability to be able to visualize, frame and recreate our world.** We live in a fallen world and our imaginative ability is our creative ability. We are not of the world but we are here on the world. Therefore, when we do not like what we are seeing in our lives, we must always remember that the ability to change it resides in us.

We can create what we want with our creative abilities when we first see it with the eyes of our spirits and then speak it forth. We must keep saying it while following the leading of the Holy Spirit. As long as our desires are in line with the provisions of the Gospel of Christ, we do not stop confessing it until we have what we are saying. The Lord Jesus said that we would have our confessed results, so let us trust Him and not change our confessions no matter how long it takes us to get them manifested. God is faithful and He can never fail us because His Word never fails. If it failed, it was not the Word of God. See the certainty of God's promises in these verses of Scripture in Hebrews 6:16-20

> *"For men verily swear by the greater: and an oath for confirmation is to them an end of all strife. Wherein God, willing more abundantly to shew unto the heirs of promise the immutability of his counsel, confirmed it by an oath: That by two immutable things, in which it was impossible for God to lie, we might have a strong consolation, who have fled for refuge to lay hold upon the hope set before us: Which hope we have as an anchor of the soul, both sure and stedfast, and which entereth into that within the veil; Whither the forerunner is for us entered, even Jesus, made an high priest for ever after the order of Melchisedec."*

Always remember that God is good, faithful, kind, and that He has called us to a life of glory, virtue, honor, dignity and excellence. Hear what God tells us in **2 Peter 1:3-4**:

> *"According as his divine power hath given unto us all things that pertain unto life and godliness, through the knowledge of him that hath called us to glory and virtue: Whereby are given unto us exceeding great and precious promises: that by these ye might be partakers of the divine nature, having escaped the corruption that is in the world through lust."*

He made us His children on earth because of His Son's finished work; His express image; the outshining or effulgence of His glory just like Christ Jesus our Lord. Therefore, let us continue to behold His glory in His Word and be transformed into the glory that we see in His Word. **2 Corinthians 3:18** —*"But we all, with open face beholding as in a glass the glory of the Lord, are changed into the same image from glory to glory, even as by the Spirit of the Lord."* We are the glory of God and our lives are designed for His glory. When we continually look into the Mirror of God (His Word) that is given to us in the Bible, we will be transformed and positioned by His Spirit in us for an extraordinary life of dominion on earth. These are absolute statements, yet they are real. Let us "arise and shine for our light is come" by Christ's resurrection. The glory of the LORD is risen upon us in spite of the darkness that is in the world today.

Yes, His glory is risen upon us true believers in Him. Therefore, arise, shine child of God. It is our Father's desire for us. Hear Him in **Isaiah 60:1-6**:

> *"Arise, shine; for thy light is come, and the glory of the LORD is risen upon thee. For, behold, the darkness shall cover the earth, and gross darkness the people: but the LORD shall arise upon thee, and his glory shall be seen upon thee. And the Gentiles shall come to thy light, and kings to the brightness of thy rising. Lift up thine eyes round about, and see: all they gather themselves together, they come to thee: thy sons shall come from far, and thy daughters shall be nursed at thy side. Then thou shalt see, and flow together, and thine heart shall fear, and be enlarged; because the abundance of the sea shall be converted unto thee, the forces of the Gentiles shall come unto thee. The multitude of camels shall cover thee, the dromedaries of Midian and Ephah; all they from Sheba shall come: they shall bring gold and incense; and they shall shew forth the praises of the LORD."*

We are God's "spiritual Israel" today and these scriptures belong to us now. We can activate them in our lives and circumstances by personalizing and speaking them forth. **Christians are designed to function by the Word of God and not by a moral code.** The Word of God is a person and He lives in every believer in Him. He is actually the one doing all we need to do when we let Him as we see in **John 1:1-5**:

> *"In the beginning was the Word, and the Word was with God, and the Word was God. The same was in the beginning with God. All things were made by him; and without him was not anything made that was made. In him was life; and the life was the light*

of men. And the light shineth in darkness; and the darkness comprehended it not."

According to **Colossians 1:26-28**, Christ Jesus is in every true believer and every true believer is in Him — *"Even the mystery which hath been hid from ages and from generations, but now is made manifest to his saints: To whom God would make known what is the riches of the glory of this mystery among the Gentiles; which is Christ in you, the hope of glory: Whom we preach, warning every man, and teaching every man in all wisdom; that we may present every man perfect in Christ Jesus."*

We learn in scriptures in **Romans 8:29-33** that we are conformed to His image — *"For whom he did foreknow, he also did predestinate to be conformed to the image of his Son, that he might be the firstborn among many brethren. Moreover whom he did predestinate, them he also called: and whom he called, them he also justified: and whom he justified, them he also glorified"* It does not matter what is going on in the world we live, we can carry out our God-given assignments of establishing His will on earth. This is because, through His Spirit that is in us, we are one with Him and He has ordered everything to function in our favor— *"And we know that all things work together for good to them that love God, to them who are the called according to his purpose... What shall we then say to these things? If God be for us, who can be against us? He that spared not his own Son, but delivered him up for us all, how shall he not with him also freely give us all things? Who shall lay anything to the charge of God's elect? It is God that justifieth."*

We are who He has made us; His ambassadors on earth representing His Kingdom as outlined in 2 Corinthians 5:20-21 — *"Now then we are ambassadors for Christ, as though God did beseech you by us: we pray you in Christ's stead, be ye reconciled to God. For he hath made him to be sin for us, who knew no sin; that we might be made the righteousness of God in him."* We are expected to cooperate with the Holy Spirit and to do the job of making His will to be done on earth as it is done in heaven. This is very significant because God functions on the earth only through men. Child of God, take God seriously. He commissioned us and gave us a mandate. *"And Jesus came and spake unto them, saying, All power is given unto me in heaven and in earth Go ye therefore, and teach all nations, baptizing them in the name of the Father, and of the Son, and of the Holy Ghost: Teaching them to observe all things whatsoever I have commanded you: and, lo, I am with you alway, even unto the end of the world. Amen."* We have a God-given job to do on earth. Our Christianity does not just consist in our profession that we are Christians and in our church attendance. There is much more to being a Christian than that. We have a gospel to preach that reveals the Christ in us; that shows us forth as the express image of His person and the effulgence of His glory. Jesus lived on earth to glorify God, and that should be our desire, passion, and pursuit in life as well. We must be conscious always that we are on earth, for the purpose of revealing Christ to our world. Our goal in life, therefore should be that, everywhere we go, and in everything we do, Christ should be exalted in and through us by the power of His Spirit. We must also be mindful of the fact that as Christians, we are going to give account of how well we did our God- given jobs here on earth, when time will be no more. This is why the Holy Spirit alerts us in 2Corinthians 5:5-10:

> *"God is the one who has prepared us for this change, and he gave us his Spirit as the guarantee of all that he has in store for us. So we are always full of courage. We know that as long as we are at home in the body we are away from the Lord's home. For our life is a matter of faith, not of sight. We are full of courage and would much prefer to leave our home in the body and be at home with the Lord. More than anything else, however, we want to please him, whether in our home here or there. For all of us must appear before Christ, to be judged by him. **We will each receive what we deserve, according to everything we have done, good or bad, in our bodily life."***

Make this confession: My spirit, soul, and body are completely under the Lordship and dominion of the Lord Jesus Christ. He has gained preeminence over my life, and His divine will and purpose are fulfilled in and through my life. My life is the expression of the glory of God. Christ is exalted in me; His divinity is manifested through me today, as I live to fulfill His purpose and do His perfect will! Thank You Father, for Your wisdom, ability, and power, that are inherent in me, in Jesus' Name. Amen.

Chapter Three

RENEW YOUR MIND WITH THE WORD OF GOD

Dear believer in Christ Jesus, you can change your world. How? We are told in **Proverbs 23:7** that as a man thinks in his heart so is he —*"For as he thinketh in his heart, so is he."* **Thoughts are powerful. What are your thoughts? What are you thinking and seeing in your mind concerning that matter or situation.** The mind is the battle ground but God gave it to us as a winning tool, with His Word in our hearts! When we win in our minds, we have won in the situation. Therefore, renew your mind with the Word of God so that you can think the thoughts of God. This is what God wants and wills us to do. To illustrate this point, take a look at **Romans 12:1-2** below:

> *"I beseech you therefore, brethren, by the mercies of God, that ye present your bodies a living sacrifice, holy, acceptable unto God, which is* your reasonable service. And be not conformed to this world: but be ye transformed by the renewing of your mind, that ye may prove what is that good, and acceptable, and perfect, will of God."*

Educate your spirit with the Word of God as you have trained or educated your intellect. If you did not train your intellect, you would not have become the professional that you are today; you would have been an illiterate man or woman. Why then would you want to be an illiterate person spiritually? If you profess Christ as Lord, you have to know Him intimately through His Spirit and His Word. This knowledge will empower you to function rightly in His Kingdom. If intellectual illiteracy is expensive, you can calculate how utterly foolish and dangerous it is for a believer in Christ to be a spiritual illiterate. There is an enemy out there, his name is Satan. He has a hierarchy of demonic forces or wicked spirits and they are here on earth. Check out these scriptures below because they tell us some things about the enemy of our souls —**Revelation 12:9**:

> *"And the great dragon was cast out, that old serpent, called the Devil, and Satan, which deceiveth the whole world: he was cast out into the earth, and his angels were cast out with him."*

Ephesians 6:10-18:

> *"Finally, my brethren, be strong in the Lord, and in the power of his might. Put on the whole armor of God that ye may be able to stand against the wiles of the devil. For we wrestle not against flesh and blood, but against principalities, against powers, against the rulers of the darkness of this world, against spiritual wickedness in high places. Wherefore take unto you the whole armor of God that ye may be able to withstand in the evil day, and having done all, to stand. Stand therefore, having your loins girt about with truth, and having on the breastplate of righteousness; And your feet shod with the preparation of the gospel of peace. Above all, taking the shield of faith, wherewith ye shall be able to quench all the fiery darts of the wicked. And take the helmet of salvation, and the sword of the Spirit, which is the word of God: Praying always with all prayer and supplication in*

the Spirit, and watching thereunto with all perseverance and supplication for all saints."

When we are clothed with the full armor of God and we are spiritually educated, Satan and all his cohorts; both human and demonic forces do not count. The spiritually illiterate Christian however, does not know what to do when the enemy of the brethren attacks. This can be a very dangerous and pitiable position to be in. This type of suffering at the hands of the devil and his cohorts is unnecessary. In **Matthew 28:18-20**, we see the power and authority that the Lord Jesus has delegated to us:

"...Jesus came and spake unto them, saying, All power is given unto me in heaven and in earth. Go ye therefore, and teach all nations, baptizing them in the name of the Father, and of the Son, and of the Holy Ghost: Teaching them to observe all things whatsoever I have commanded you: and, lo, I am with you alway, even unto the end of the world. Amen."

We must be very conscious of His ever abiding presence and take advantage of it by relating with Him through His Spirit who lives in us forever. **When we are conscious of whose we are, who we are, and who we carry inside of us, the devil will not be a factor at all, but know that your thoughts form your words.** What are you seeing in your mind concerning that matter? Are you seeing what God has said concerning the situation? Or you are seeing and saying what the devil is showing you about the circumstance? You can only see what God has said if you know what God has said in the matter. <u>This is why we must educate our spirits to live victoriously in this life through the Spirit and the Word</u>. **Once you voice what the situation is showing you, your words create and they determine the way your life goes. You may not know it, but there are positive and negative forces that are ready to do what you are saying in the spiritual realm and it will be manifest in the physical realm.** Therefore, be careful who you empower on your behalf.

You have to learn to agree with what God has said concerning you no matter the circumstantial evidence. **In the face of apparent defeat, decree and declare that you are a victor in Christ.** Even when the pain becomes very intense; decree and declare that *"by His stripes I am healed."* If I was healed then, I am healed now and I take my healing right now. I am the healed of God; therefore, I refuse to be sick because I live in divine health. Hallelujah! I can never forget one Tuesday morning in August 2008 when my husband suffered a stroke and became paralyzed on his right side and could neither stand nor walk. We knew what to do so we took the Word of God and started declaring all the healing scriptures. We kept making faith declarations all day Tuesday, Wednesday and by Thursday, he could stand and walk by holding onto the wall!

We trusted God's Word and kept on declaring and acting on it. By Friday morning, he was able to stand and to walk without holding onto to the wall. Then, we went to see his doctor. The doctor did not have much to do because the inherent power in the Word of God had taken care of the situation. He was healed and there were no signs that he ever had such a serious stoke. Therefore, you have to learn to focus on the Word and not on the circumstantial evidence and as a result, you will receive what you see and say. **The Lord Jesus gave us the victory to enjoy our stay here on earth. When we finally relocate to heaven, it will be a continuous celebration. There is nothing to be victorious over in heaven but on earth, we have to establish the victorious life that we have been given in Christ through the Holy Spirit and the Word.**

When we educate our human spirits in the things of the Spirit, we will know what to do when the storms of life blow our way. When we live from our spirits, we are living from victory to victory and from glory to glory because the Greater One lives in us and we know how to take advantage of His presence in us. As we decree and declare the Word, the Holy Spirit will bring to pass our faith declarations. We must voice our faith. **The Word of God is the Light of God.** Just as God said in Genesis one, *"Let there be light: and there was light,"* we can also decree, "let there be light" and light will come on in that area of our lives where there was darkness.

Through faith proclamation of God's Word, we are more than conquerors and we conquer darkness as we release the light which drives away the forces of darkness. Beloved, start proclaiming the light of God's Word today; we must proclaim light before darkness can flee. What are you doing to shine in His glory? We were called from darkness to light and to proclaim the light of God's Word. We see in **1 Peter 2:9-10** below, who God says we are. We cannot afford to live below our calling by being ignorant of God's Word concerning us:

> *"But ye are a chosen generation, a royal priesthood, an holy nation, a peculiar people; that ye should shew forth the praises of him who hath called you out of darkness into his marvelous light: Which in time past were not a people, but are now the people of God: which had not obtained mercy, but now have obtained mercy." Hallelujah!*

He who has called and chosen us in Himself is faithful. He is the Vine and we are His branches. Therefore, we are indivisibly one with Him. Hear the Lord in these verses of scriptures in **John 15: 1-9** because wisdom demands that we take heed to divine counsel:

> *"I am the true vine, and my Father is the husbandman. Every branch in me that beareth not fruit he taketh away: and every branch that beareth fruit, he purgeth it, that it may bring forth more fruit. Now ye are clean through the word which I have spoken unto you.* ***Abide in me, and I in you. As the branch cannot bear fruit of itself, except it abide in the vine; no more can ye, except ye abide in me. I am the vine, ye are the branches: He that abideth in me, and I in him, the same bringeth forth much fruit: for without me ye can do nothing. If a man abide not in me, he is cast forth as a branch, and is withered; and men gather them, and cast them into the fire, and they are burned. If ye abide in me, and***

> *<u>my words abide in you, ye shall ask what ye will, and it shall be done unto you. Herein is my Father glorified, that ye bear much fruit; so shall ye be my disciples. As the Father hath loved me, so have I loved you: continue ye in my love.</u>"*

The branches (us) beautify the Vine (Christ) but the branches are nourished by the Vine. They produce flowers and then fruits but, there is no stress on their part. **It is all by His grace**. All God is asking us to do is to increase in our knowledge of Him so that we will be fruitful in every area of our lives as stated in **2 Peter 1:2-4**:

> "<u>Grace and peace be multiplied unto you through the knowledge of God, and of Jesus our Lord, According as his divine power hath given unto us all things that pertain unto life and godliness, through the knowledge of him that hath called us to glory and virtue:</u> Whereby are given unto us exceeding great and precious promises: <u>that by these ye might be partakers of the divine nature, having escaped the corruption that is in the world through lust.</u>"

The Lord Jesus Christ is the Light of the world. He is also the Sun of Righteousness as revealed to us in **Malachi 4:2** —*"But unto you that fear my name shall the Sun of righteousness arise with healing in his wings; and ye shall go forth, and grow up as calves of the stall."* He is our Source and we reflect His glory wherever we are. He designed us by His Spirit for productivity and effectiveness in all that we do because we are rooted in Him. We need to take a close look at our lives in order to determine how much of God's expectations of us we are meeting in our earthly walk. God has not called us to a life of struggle or of suffering. We need very much to renew our minds with His Word when we find ourselves struggling in life. Failure to grow in the knowledge of Him shows that we are frustrating His grace in our lives. Therefore, the lack and struggles in our lives show that there is something we are supposed to be doing that we are not doing because God said in **Hosea 4:6**:

"<u>My people are destroyed for lack of knowledge: because thou hast rejected knowledge, I will also reject thee,</u> that thou shalt be no priest to me: seeing thou hast forgotten the law of thy God, I will also forget thy children."

Only fools ignore Knowledge. Information brings knowledge and knowledge brings power. **How informed are you in the things of the Spirit?** The Holy Spirit said in **Proverbs 13:16**, *"Every prudent man dealeth with knowledge: but a fool layeth open his folly."* The lord Jesus Christ has been made unto us wisdom. Therefore, He is our wisdom and He is our life and our ability. We cannot afford to ignore Him and expect to fulfill our calling.

We must always remember that we are a chosen generation called to reveal His glory. When this is not the case, then, it is time to stop and take stock of our lives. It is then time for us to ask ourselves some heart searching questions. Is my mind renewed with the information provided for me in the scriptures? Have I been a fool by ignoring the knowledge and instruction of God's Word? **Proverbs 1:7** says, *"The fear of the LORD is the beginning of knowledge: but fools despise wisdom and instruction."* How much of the knowledge of God do I have in my spirit? Do I really Know Him or do I just know about Him? He is the Vine and am I connected to Him? Am I rooted in Him? Do I have the life sap of the Vine flowing in me and nourishing me? Am I expecting His return? When your answer is yes to these questions, then you can declare that Christ has come into your life and that you are fruitful in every good work in accordance with **Colossians 1:9-20:**

"For this cause we also, since the day we heard it, do not cease to pray for you, and to desire that ye might be filled with the knowledge of his will in all wisdom and spiritual understanding; That ye might walk worthy of the Lord unto all pleasing, being fruitful in every good work, and increasing in the knowledge of God; Strengthened with all might, according to his glorious power, unto all patience and longsuffering

with joyfulness; Giving thanks unto the Father, which hath made us meet to be partakers of the inheritance of the saints in light: Who hath delivered us from the power of darkness, and hath translated us into the kingdom of his dear Son: In whom we have redemption through his blood, even the forgiveness of sins:

Who is the image of the invisible God, the firstborn of every creature: For by him were all things created, that are in heaven, and that are in earth, visible and invisible, whether they be thrones, or dominions, or principalities, or powers: all things were created by him, and for him: And he is before all things, and by him all things consist. And he is the head of the body, the church: who is the beginning, the firstborn from the dead; that in all things he might have the preeminence. For it pleased the Father that in him should all fullness dwell; And, having made peace through the blood of his cross, by him to reconcile all things unto himself; by him, I say, whether they be things in earth, or things in heaven."

Christ has completed His work and He loves us that have personally put our trust in Him and in His finished work. How are you taking advantage of what He achieved and provided for our enjoyment? True life and enjoyment can only be found in Christ Jesus. Beloved, if you are not confidently sure of the answers to the questions above, you surely need to renew your mind by the help of the Holy Spirit and with the Word of God.

Make this confession: I belong to my Lord Jesus Christ who gave me eternal life- the overcoming, indestructible, unconquerable life of God; and I walk with this consciousness today; knowing that I am not of this world. I am not at all subject to the circumstances and rudiments of this earthly realm. I am a victor in Christ Jesus. Greater is He that is in me than he that is in the world. The Word of faith that changes things is in my heart and in my mouth today, prevailing over circumstances and situations in the Name of Jesus. Satan and his cohorts are under my feet; and I live perpetually in victory, divine health, dominion, and righteousness, in Jesus' Name. Amen.

CHAPTER FOUR

AGREE WITH GOD

God has counseled us to renew our minds with His Word by the help of His Spirit. He said we should abide in Him and we must agree with Him. Agreeing with His Word and speaking God's promises can bring about His amazing blessings and cause His will to be done in our lives and on earth. **What is God's testimony concerning us? It is in His written Word —the logos of God.** When we agree with God and speak forth what He has already testified concerning us, the Holy Spirit has the legal right to act on our behalf. He assigns the angels of God to get busy on our behalf. Therefore, we have to learn how to keep our angels busy by dispatching them to do what God has assigned them to do for us with our words. They are assigned to us as "ministering spirits" to minister for us because we are heirs of salvation. We see this stated in **Hebrews 1:14**:

> *"Are they not all ministering spirits, sent forth to minister for them who shall be heirs of salvation?"*

Always remember that what we say is what we get. For example, when we spend just ten minutes a day in confessing and declaring the truth of God's Word over our lives, thereby programming our day and our lives for success, we will be amazed at what happens. **Christianity is for Talkers.** <u>If you do not say it, your spirit cannot take a hold of it.</u> For The Lord Jesus said in Mark 11:23 that you shall have what you say, it is a spiritual law, and also **Romans 10:13** (MSG) says, *"Everyone who calls, 'Help, God!' Gets help."*

Paul said in **2 Corinthians 4:13** that *"We having the same spirit of faith, according as it is written, I believed, and therefore have spoken; we also believe, and therefore speak."* Declaring what you already know and believe with all your heart surely does strengthen your spirit man. Your declaration makes the Word which you declare to become active in your life. Our decrees and faith declarations cause changes and transformations in our lives which then position us to enjoy all the provisions of the Gospel of Christ Jesus. We release our faith by declaring that we already have them. In other words, we call those things that are not as though they are and they become — we see the manifestation of whatever we are saying in the physical! Our lives go in the direction of what we are saying because we have what we say. It is ours already but we seize it by faith because Colossians 1:27 tells us that Christ is in us — He is our everything; consciously agree with God's Word and make Jesus Christ first in your life. Why should you do that? The reason is because He was and He is first in everything.

- "He was Mary's firstborn son (Luke 2:7).
- He is the firstborn among all brothers and sisters (Rom. 8:29).
- He is the firstborn over all creation (Col. 1:15).
- He is the firstborn *among* the dead (Col. 1:18).
- He is the firstborn *from* the dead (Rev. 1:5).
- He is the first and the last (Rev. 1:17).
- He is the Alpha and Omega (Rev. 1:8).
- He is the beginning and the end (Rev. 22:13).
- He is the King of kings and Lord of lords (Rev. 19:16).
- Every knee in heaven, on earth and under the earth will bow before Him (Phil. 2:10)."

This means that everything our hearts desire is in us because we are in Him who is first in everything, who is everything and He is in us. Therefore we have everything we need in Him. Thus, all we need to do is call them forth. It is a Kingdom principle and we have to practice it if we want to enjoy the Kingdom life on earth. **Jesus**

came that we might have life to the full but our words create the atmosphere in which we operate our lives. When you talk health, you live in an atmosphere of health. When you talk abundance, you also live in an atmosphere of abundance. The contrary is also true. **There is a miracle in your mouth waiting for an opportunity to come into existence when you speak it forth. You are in charge of what you allow in your space on earth.** I suggest that we take out time every day to practice some talking sessions: boldly declaring in faith, the mind of God (the Word of God) concerning us in Christ. **The creative power is in the Word of God and it is released by speaking it forth.**

We will be blessed in our faithfulness and consistency! The blessings belong to the doers so let us release the power of God's Word to work for us! We must water our spiritual clouds with our faith declarations of what God has said concerning us in His Word. There will be abundance of the rain of God's multiple blessings poured out upon us when our clouds are over-saturated. This is a significant God's Kingdom principle for us to live by today. The wisdom and power in God's Word will direct us in all that we do when we are full of His Word. The Holy Spirit said in **Colossians 3:16** that we should allow the Word of Christ to dwell richly in our hearts —*"Let the word of Christ dwell in you richly in all wisdom; teaching and admonishing one another in psalms and hymns and spiritual songs, singing with grace in your hearts to the Lord."* To create, God meditated; He knew what He wanted and He spoke it forth. Yes! It came to pass as He spoke it! He said, *"Let there be light and there was light!"*

Check God's creation history in the Bible for yourself in the second chapter of this book. You can also go to Genesis Chapter One in the Bible to see it for yourself. Jesus said that you shall have what you say. God's Word is the only truth we should know and accept. No matter what is going on, speak the Word of God to the situation; the Word always prevails. Since delay is not denial, patiently keep talking the Word until you have what you say. Never give up; giving up too soon will make you to forsake your mercy. Speak into being what you want to prevail in your ministry, life, home and business.

Keep saying it. Murmuring and complaining will only displease God and empower the forces of darkness against you.

Speak God's Word continually and see God's perfect will come to pass in all that concerns you because He has perfected us and all that concerns us. Meditate on these scriptures and appreciate what God has done for us in His Son, Jesus Christ our Lord, as stated in **Hebrews 10:14-25**:

> *"**For by one offering he hath perfected forever them that are sanctified.** Whereof the Holy Ghost also is a witness to us: for after that he had said before, This is the covenant that I will make with them **after those days, saith the Lord, I will put my laws into their hearts, and in their minds will I write them; And their sins and iniquities will I remember no more.** Now where remission of these is, there is no more offering for sin. **Having therefore, brethren, boldness to enter into the holiest by the blood of Jesus, By a new and living way, which he hath consecrated for us, through the veil, that is to say, his flesh; And having an high priest over the house of God; Let us draw near with a true heart in full assurance of faith, having our hearts sprinkled from an evil conscience, and our bodies washed with pure water.***
>
> *Let us hold fast the profession of our faith without wavering; (for he is faithful that promised; And let us consider one another to provoke unto love and to good works: Not forsaking the assembling of ourselves together, as the manner of some is; **but exhorting one another: and so much the more, as ye see the day approaching**."*

God is not about to do what He said He has done; it is done already and glory to His holy Name! We have been cleansed and we are now with Christ in God. Hear the Holy Spirit describe and instruct the true believer in Christ Jesus in **Colossians 3:1-3**:

> ***"If ye then be risen with Christ, seek those things which are above,*** *where Christ sitteth on the right hand of God. Set your affection on things above, not on things on the earth. For ye are dead, and your life is hid with Christ in God."*

Agree with God and cooperate with His Spirit whom He has placed in us to be our very present help in time of need. See this in **Psalm 46:1-5**:

> ***"God is our refuge and strength, a very present help in trouble.*** *Therefore will not we fear, though the earth be removed, and though the mountains be carried into the midst of the sea; Though the waters thereof roar and be troubled, though the mountains shake with the swelling thereof. Selah. There is a river, the streams whereof shall make glad the city of God, the holy place of the tabernacles of the most High. God is in the midst of her; she shall not be moved:* **God shall help her, and that right early**.*"*

You see, we have no reason whatsoever to fret or to be anxious about anything in this world that we are passing through. Start sowing the right seeds as you make your daily faith declarations. They will produce the fruits of what they talk about in your life, ministry, family and business because they are God's Word. There are power and life in God's Word and they give it the ability to change hopeless situations and cause circumstances to conform to God's plans and purposes for us. This happens when we activate the inherent power of the Word by faith –that is, by speaking, acting on the Word and applying it always no matter what. When you speak the Word in faith, the Spirit of God incubates it and brings it to pass. He takes a hold together with us to make it happen as we are declaring. This is God's way of doing things for us and with us on earth, but He does not do it alone because He does it with our cooperation.

The Lord Jesus Christ is the Living Word of God and He has been made unto us Peace and Wisdom. The Word of God does not and can never fail because God never fails. **The Word of God is God.** Therefore, you need to spend time in the Word of God and cultivate the presence of the Holy Spirit in your everyday life in Christ. You need to draw whatever you need from Him on a daily basis because He is our strength and life. His ability is our ability. He will guide and direct your life according to God's destiny for you. As a result, you will never fall. <u>The Spirit of God will give you more Words to declare as you are consistent in these talking sessions because He sticks closer than a brother</u>. He is our Helper, our Comforter, our Guide, our Guard, our Counselor, our Teacher and our Strengthener from within. In fact, He is our all in all. He helps us to do all things. Without His help, we cannot do anything that is acceptable to God our Father. We should therefore yield to and depend on the Holy Spirit for everything we need to do as believers.

While on earth, the Lord said that He could do nothing without the Father. Hear Him in **John 5:19-31**:

> *"Then answered Jesus and said unto them, Verily, verily, I say unto you, **<u>The Son can do nothing of himself, but what he seeth the Father do: for what things soever he doeth, these also doeth the Son likewise... I can of mine own self do nothing: as I hear, I judge: and my judgment is just; because I seek not mine own will, but the will of the Father which hath sent me</u>**. If I bear witness of myself, my witness is not true."*

How can we who are now on earth do without the Father and the Holy Spirit who lives in us? He is the One who does the works of God the Father, who is in heaven, on the earth today. Just as our Lord was able to see what the Father was doing, we can also see what the Father is doing in the now of our lives when we look into the mirror of God's Word. The Holy Spirit will reveal God to us in His Word and change us into the glory that we see in the Word of God; hallelujah! Beloved, boldly decree and declare the Word of God daily in faith concerning every area of your life and ministry in order to create the realities you want to see in your life and circumstances.

Remember that the Lord Jesus said that what we say is what comes to us. In other words, what we say is what we get. Therefore, we have to agree with God and speak what He has said concerning our finances, jobs, businesses, families, ministries, health and where we will spend eternity. Then, act and live that way.

For the Word of faith is in our mouths to command situations and circumstances of life to conform to God's destiny for our lives. The power to change what we do not like dwells in us. **Therefore, as we declare faith filled words, solutions to life challenges will abound because our Lord Jesus Christ is God's Word. He is God's ultimate "Yes."** *He always does what He says—for all of God's promises have been fulfilled in Christ with a resounding "Yes!" And through Christ, our "Amen" which means "Yes," ascends to God for His glory (2 Corinthians 1:19 b- 20 NLT).*

Load your spiritual clouds daily f*or God says, "At just the right time I heard you. On the day of salvation, I helped you." Indeed, the "right time" is now. "Today is the day of salvation"* —**2 Corinthians 6:2** (NLT).

Things are WON in the spirit realm before you see them in the natural realm. Pray the Word. What has God said concerning the matter? Search the scriptures. He is watching over His Word to perform it. Jeremiah 1:12 *"Then said Jehovah unto me, Thou hast well seen: for I watch over my word to perform it."* ASV

Therefore, make use of the Word of God by speaking it forth in prayer and declare it, in order to take possession of what is rightfully yours! **WIN IT IN THE SPIRIT AND THEN EXPECT IT IN THE NATURAL! You must maintain a love relationship with God, through His Word and by His Spirit. That is what Christianity is all about. Talk with God, He is a person and He loves you completely. Speak out loud what He has told you. Virtually live in it.** The Word of God that is spoken ministers to us on the inside in such a powerful way that it begins to show up in our lives. We need to be speaking His Word if we are going to experience the fullness of His grace and be ministers of His grace to the world.

The confession of God's Word applies "Truth Pressure" to our hearts. God's Word is filled with divine influence (grace) that feeds and strengthens our spirit man until that truth shows up in our souls and bodies and is reflected in our lives for all to see. **Change will always come first in our hearts before we see it manifest in the natural. My Pastor taught me that I must first prevail with God, before I can prevail with man. How true! This can only be done by my total dependence on God alone to help me by His Spirit and His Word in my earth walk.**

I pray for you, beloved of God:
May God our Father, The Lord Jesus Christ and the Holy Spirit give you love, grace and communion to be all God the Father desires you to be; all that He paid such a Supreme Price to accomplish by sacrificing His Son. Amen in Jesus' Name.

CONCLUSION

The words we speak are containers because they have the power to bring about what we say. Why? Because there are positive and negative forces that are available in the spirit realm to enforce them. This is my counsel to you beloved of God; love God, become intimate with Him, know Him for yourself and do not just know about Him. Interact with Him through His Spirit as your loving Heavenly Father who loves you with an everlasting love that is complete and perfect. Speak His Word over you daily and your life will be upwards and forwards only. **His Word is working every time and everywhere!**

Do not take lightly what you have read in this book and other books on the same subject. Put the truth of God's Word to work and declare God's Word daily. Spend quality time in communion and fellowship with the Holy Spirit by reading, studying, meditating on the Word and by hearing from God in your quiet time with Him and His Word. Afterwards, declare and act upon what God communicated to your spirit while you were alone in His presence. Live by God's **WORD** and you will be amazed at how exciting the Christian life truly is. I want you to know that the quality of your life on earth depends on your perception of God. You can only know God through His Word by His Spirit. This is the only way you can have a correct perception of who God really is and how much He loves you. Your discovery, will position you to love and enjoy God, living only to please Him. Then, you can learn to talk God's talk and to pay attention to what is coming out of your mouth— *"The mouth of* *the righteous is a well of life, But violence covers the mouth of the wicked"* (***Proverb 10:11***).

Remember, it is our spiritual responsibility to educate our spirits to be able to enforce the perfect will of God in our lives and in our world. It is our God-given duty. Just as you were zealous about passing your professional exams, use the same zeal and more to study the Word of God in order to show yourself approved; a workman that needs not to be ashamed but rightly dividing the Word of truth. The activities that take place in our spirits are mostly what govern our lives. In other words, what we store in our spirits will determine our successes or failures in life because according to **Proverbs 4:23**, *"out of your spirit are the issues of life."*

The world's measurement of success is very different from God's measurement of success. <u>Good success is not based on just how well you are doing naturally</u>. **By God's standard, "success" must be an all-round success in your spirit, soul and body.** See His desire for us in **3 John 2-4**:

> *"Beloved, I wish above all things that thou mayest prosper and be in health, even as thy soul prospereth. For I rejoiced greatly, when the brethren came and testified of the truth that is in thee, even as thou walkest in the truth. I have no greater joy than to hear that my children walk in truth."*

Educate your spirit with the Word of God; know the truth and it will be your sure guide as you navigate this world. **The Word of God works every time and everywhere for whosoever will work it by the help of the Holy Spirit.** It will grow, develop mightily and prevail in your life and circumstances when you put it into your spirit to program your life.

WHAT TO DO

Below are some daily faith declarations that you can start with. Declare what you have been made in Christ to be and see your life and circumstances manifest these truths. You may be thinking that these declarations do not exactly match what you are experiencing in your life right now, but do not worry about it because God understands and knows exactly where you are concerning your situation. With your declaration, He wants you to give Him the legal right to make you all what His Word says you are. **This is why you have to practice the Kingdom principles of faith in the God who gives life to the dead and calls into existence the things that do not exist; by daily speaking forth these faith declarations.** They will become faith realities for you.

God gave us His Word that we might boldly say what He has said concerning us in order to bring them to pass in our lives. Therefore, we need to have the mentality of the Word of God. We do this by storing the Word in our spirits. This enables us to bring every wrong thought into captivity and "talk up" (stir) our spirits with the Word. In return, this gives us the spiritual sense to deal with the issues of life. Beloved, I know by being taught the Word and by experience that the Word works every time and everywhere for whosoever will agree with God and walk with Him in His Word and through His Spirit. Therefore, I have made up my mind to walk the path of victory, success and prosperity by the Word and by the Spirit of the Living God.

I know who I am through the Word; I am royalty! I belong to a chosen race, a royal priesthood, a holy nation and a peculiar people. God has set me apart to show forth His wonderful deeds. I am displaying through the Holy Spirit who lives in me, the virtues and perfections of the One who has called me out of darkness into His marvelous light. I agree with God's Spirit and I dwell in God's marvelous light —I am shining!

I do not know what you have chosen to do but I suggest that you choose to allow the Holy Spirit to lead you. That is where true and good success lies; on this side of heaven and for eternity. Therefore, be faithful and consistent in your walk with God. When He sees your faithful and consistent faith declarations, the Holy Spirit will give you fresh ones on a daily basis. It does not matter what you see, what you hear or what you feel now; it does not matter how negative or impossible things look in the natural, just keep declaring the Word! Do not stop "talking it" <u>until you are</u> or <u>until you have</u> what the Word talks about. The Word of faith in your mouth produces results.

All things are yours according to 1 Corinthians 3:21 and everything you need is inside you —the Holy Spirit and the Word! In 2008, we needed to buy a land for our church. We found one but we did not have the money to buy it at the time so we applied the Kingdom principle of *"calling those things that be not as if they were."* This is what we are talking about here. We declared that the land was ours and we called forth the money. By June 2009, we bought the land and fully paid for it! The Word of God is working every time and everywhere.

<u>Your blessings have your name tags on them in the heavenly places in Christ</u>. **Therefore, it is your responsibility to activate your harvest by your faith. It is not God's responsibility to ensure that you are enjoying all that He has blessed you with in Christ. It is our job to do something with what He has already given to us in Christ through His Spirit.** The Spirit of God indwells you as a genuine believer in Christ Jesus and He relies on your faith to operate on your behalf on earth so that God's will can be done for you on earth as it is done in heaven. **In the mind of God, <u>you are</u> and <u>you have</u> all that He has made you and given you in Christ.** He is not aware you are sick or broke. As far as God is concerned,

you are His heir and a joint-heir with Christ. Therefore, in the mind of God, you are healthy and wealthy.

The "I" in the Daily Faith Declarations segments of the next pages is you talking the Word and not just the author. You are developing the mentality of the Word of God and you will have what you say and become what you say. Refuse to consider circumstances or recognize impossibilities but focus on the Word and what is being said concerning you. Function from your spiritually recreated and educated human spirit and be of good cheer because the Word works every time and everywhere for everyone who would dare to believe and trust God. The Lord Jesus asked in **John 11:40** (NET), *"Didn't I tell you if you believe, you would see the glory of God?"*

The Prayer of Salvation

He also said in **Mark 9:23** (KJV), *"If thou canst believe, all things are possible to him that believeth."* So, believe and declare that the Word of God is true and that it has inherent power; it works every time and everywhere! If you are not a Christian yet, or you are not assured of your salvation and you are reading this book, blessed are you for God so loved you that He gave His Son in your place on the Cross. All you need to do now is pray this simple prayer of salvation and you will become a part of all that God is saying in this book. Pray this prayer and mean it with all your heart:

"O Lord God, I come to You in the Name of Jesus Christ. Your Word says, in **Acts 2:21** that, *"... Whosoever shall call on the name of the Lord shall be saved."* Therefore, I ask Jesus to come into my heart to be the Lord of my life. I receive eternal life into my spirit and according to **Romans 10:9**, *"That if thou shalt confess with thy mouth the Lord Jesus, and shalt believe in thine heart that God hath raised Him from the dead, thou shalt be saved,"* I declare that I am saved; I am born again; I am a child of God! I have received eternal life into my spirit and I now have Christ dwelling in me — greater is He that is in me than he that is in the world (1 John 4:4)! I will now walk in the consciousness of my new life in Christ Jesus. Hallelujah!"

Congratulations saint of God! The Lord Jesus Christ has by His finished work qualified you for life in His eternal presence and at His right hand; where there is fullness of joy and pleasures forever. Enjoy your life in Christ for the Lord Himself said in **Luke 12:32** *"Fear not, little flock; for it is your Father's good pleasure to give you the kingdom."* We are on planet earth; every one of us, on God's assignments. According to **Jeremiah 1:9**, God has put His Words in our mouths — *"Then the LORD put forth his hand, and touched my mouth. And the LORD said unto me, Behold, I have put my words in thy mouth."* Therefore, we must prepare for our divine assignments because in the Kingdom of God, our preparation determines our performance. Get full of the Spirit and the Word, saint of God, and you will fulfill your God-given assignments. God bless you.
 –Pastor Mary...

Contact Information
For any inquiries, you can contact us at Christ Embassy Owings Mills, MD. 410-206-6385.

FAITH DECLARATIONS

The primary purpose of words is not communication but to release creative power — communication is secondary. So say it to believe it. When you keep saying it long enough, you will believe it. What you believe will change what you see. It's time to speak and effect changes in your life! Declare Words Of Faith! What You Say Is What You Get! The Lord Jesus Christ said so.

Day 1

I AGREE with the Holy Spirit that today, the Lord Jesus Christ owns every soul on earth by the power of His cross. Because of God's sacrifice of Jesus on behalf of all humanity, sin, its effects and consequences should not have dominion over anyone because Jesus took our place of punishment and suffered on our behalf. In other words, God judged us in Jesus on the cross and Jesus declared, *"It is finished."* We now have the legal rights to possess everything salvation in Christ brings because they were all paid for with His shed precious blood. He has reconciled us to God — *"To wit, that God was in Christ reconciling the world unto himself, not imputing their trespasses unto them; and hath committed unto us the word of reconciliation"* (2 Corinthians 5:19).

By our faith in His resurrection and our confession of His Lordship, we receive eternal life and are justified. We are now free to serve the Lord and live gloriously for Him. Therefore, I decree and declare that the light of His glorious Gospel is dawning in the hearts of the unsaved all over the earth as they hear it daily from us believers. I come against the influence of the prince of the power of the air and I declare that his authority over them is broken; the understanding of the Gospel is granted to unbelievers and the lukewarm in Jesus' Name. I decree God's incredible blessings over my life and that of my fellow saints. We are seeing an explosion of God's goodness and a sudden widespread increase in our spiritual abilities. We are experiencing the surpassing greatness of God's favor. It is elevating us to higher levels of glory than we ever dreamed of. Explosive blessings are coming our ways in Jesus' Name. Amen.

We have the capacity to contain and express God from our spirits. All we will ever need is found in the life of God that indwells in our spirits. I am a king in Christ and where the word of the king is, there is power. My dear Heavenly Father, I thank You for giving us wisdom and revelation in the knowledge of our Lord Jesus. I believe that to know Jesus is to have grace and peace multiplied to us and that to know the Lord Jesus Christ is to receive all things pertaining to life and godliness. I also declare that to know Jesus is to know the peace that passes all understanding and true prosperity —all-round prosperity! To know Jesus is to know the overcoming and victorious life. To know Jesus is to know true joy that flows like a river. To know Jesus is know You and Your love for us. To know Jesus is to know our true worth and our eternal destiny. To know Jesus is eternal life. John 17:3. Our spirits came from You LORD; we are sustained by You and we are glad that at the end, we are coming home to be with and in You forever. Thank You Father because all You said that we have in Christ is what we truly have. The light of Your favor shines upon our ways. Hallelujah!

Day 2

I AGREE and DECREE that I am a new creation in Christ Jesus; born with the glorious life and nature of God in my spirit. I have been justified by faith and I live in the light of my new life in Christ without condemnation but as the righteousness of God in Christ Jesus. I decree that I am experiencing God's faithfulness and goodness so I do not worry about anything. I do not doubt God because I know that He is real and true. He is love; He loves me and He cares about me. I am confidently trusting in Him knowing that He has said that He will never fail me, never leave me, nor forsake me — no never! I am giving birth to every promise He has put in my heart by His Spirit and I am becoming everything He created me to be in Christ. I am the exact image of my Lord Jesus Christ. I mirror Him as "He is" and I am His icon. I share His semblance and I am His extension on earth. As His icon, I manifest His personality and character. Just by touching me, all the blessings in Christ manifest everywhere I go. I am a bundle of blessings to the world.

Precious Lord Jesus, thank You for opening my eyes to see the destitute, afflicted, brokenhearted, oppressed, sick and blind people around me. Thank You for anointing me to make them free with the Good News of Your love and grace. In You Lord, I have obtained an inheritance; being predestinated according to Your purpose when You work all things after the counsel of Your own will. Thank You Daddy for giving me grace and peace. I declare Your majesty. I proclaim that Your Name is exalted for You reign and You rule magnificently Daddy. You are victorious and Your power is shown through all the earth. Father, I proclaim that You are mighty and I lift up Your Name High for You are Holy.

In honor, in glory and in adoration, I bow before Your Throne. I receive the blessing of Your Spirit through Your Word into my life today as I proclaim Your Word in faith. My mind is renewed and my life is transformed by the inherent power of Your Word. I am growing in grace and increasing in wisdom and all my circumstances are turned around for my good in Jesus' Name. I am God's Ambassador of healing and reconciliation in my world. Precious Lord, I pray that the light of Your grace that brings salvation will shine brightly in the dark places of the earth as You unveil Your Gospel through me by Your Spirit to them. I pray Lord, that men and women in these dark places would be turned from darkness to light and become partakers of Your grace and love in Jesus' Name. Thank You Lord for Your love for all men and for all it took to save us from eternal damnation. I love You Lord and I worship You for Your grace. I thank You for bringing me into union with You, and ordaining me to be fruitful and productive in every good work, joyfully bringing forth fruits unto righteousness. I yield my heart to Your Spirit always in fellowship; in the process, Your joy abounds in my heart, and I bear much more fruits in Jesus' name. Amen. These are my declarations and they are true and they are established unto me in Jesus' Name. The light of Your favor shines upon my ways. Hallelujah!

Day 3

I DECIDE and DECREE that I have the grace that I need for today. I am full of power, strength, and determination. Therefore, nothing that I face will be too much for me because I have received the abundance of grace as well as the gift of righteousness and I reign and rule in life by Jesus Christ my Lord. I overcome every obstacle, I outlast every challenge and I come through every difficulty better off than I was before. This is because I am a branded product of God's love. He recreated me in righteousness and true holiness and He catapulted me into the Kingdom of the Son of His love. He gave me His life (Zoe), He gave me His nature of righteousness and He put His Spirit in my spirit to live in me forever. Hallelujah!

Because of the Greater One who lives in me, I am a victor and a champion forever. I am sanctified from evil so there are no mishaps or destructions on my path. In my path are life, peace, victory and prosperity. I dwell in safety and as I go out daily, the land is subdued before me. Hallelujah! The anointing and grace for increase and expansion are in my life, in my ministry, in my business and in my finances more than ever before. It is my set time for growth, increase, development and expansion in all that I do. I am Abraham's Seed so the Seed of greatness is in my spirit. It is my birth-right as the Seed of Abraham because I belong to my Lord Jesus Christ. Yes, Lord, I am what You say that I am. I am healthy, victorious, super-intelligent, prosperous, strong, influential, wealthy and rich. I am Your best. You gave birth to me in order to show me off as Your first-class being and the crown of all Your creation.

Father, thank You for calling me to display the virtues and perfections of divinity! Thank You Daddy for perfecting me for the good life! Daddy, I am Your glory and my life is for Your glory. Thank You Father for giving birth to me in Christ! I am Yours; therefore, I am a success already in all that I do through Your Spirit who indwells in me. I have in me the indestructible life so I can never be defeated. I walk in health, victory, prosperity and strength every day of my life. Lord, You are my life, my strength and the Greater

One that lives in me. Do I have any reason to worry? No! I thank You my dear Heavenly Father for granting me favor according to the riches of Your glory to be strengthened with might by Your Spirit in my inner man. I declare that I can do all things through Christ who strengthens me in Jesus' Name; Amen.

Lord, thank You for Your love that is shared abroad in my heart and thank You for loving me intimately. I love You Lord and I express my love for You as I worship You and carry out Your revelations to me daily. My faith in You is my victory. I have overcome Satan and his cohorts, and the systems of this world. I'm confident in the power and ability of Your Word, which I have believed, and by which I live, to move from glory to glory, in Jesus' Name. Amen. These are my decrees and faith declarations. They are established unto me in Jesus' Name. The light of God's favor always shines upon my ways. Hallelujah!

Day 4

I DECLARE and DECREE that it is not too late to accomplish everything God has placed in my heart and that I have not missed my window of opportunity. God has moments of favor in my future and I am God's workmanship that is created in Christ Jesus for good works which God prepared beforehand that I should walk in. I thank You my Heavenly Father for blessing and causing everything that I do to multiply and prosper exceedingly. Every day, I acknowledge Your anointing and I take advantage of Your grace for expansion, growth and development in all that I do. Everything that I do grows and prospers exceedingly. Daddy, You are preparing me right now for Your glory because You are releasing a special grace to help me accomplish every dream You have placed in my heart. This is my time to enjoy the fullness of Your favor!

The rest of my life is the best of my entire life. Father, I am passionate about the dream You have placed in my heart to be blessed and to be a blessing to others in every way. I am only interested in what You are interested in. I have entered into the glorious life You gave me in Christ through Your Spirit that lives in me. I am fulfilling the destiny that You have given me in Christ; the world is mine!

Angels are always working on my behalf because I am an heir of salvation. I live in divine health, victory, success and in prosperity every day, and in every area of my life and my ministry. Your Word is always working mightily in me and all I see is Your glory. You have a financial plan for my life because I am in partnership with You. I am a "tither," therefore, I have open heavens over my life. You are pouring me out such blessings that I do not have enough room to contain them. All nations shall call me happy and blessed. The devourer is rebuked for my sake. I am a giver therefore men are giving unto my bosom blessings with good measure, pressed down, shaken together and running over. Thank You Father for shepherding my life; I do not lack for any good thing. I thank You Father for blessing me with all the blessings in Christ Jesus. As I serve You joyfully in righteousness, peace and holiness, my life is filled with Your goodness.

Thank You Father that Your wisdom is at work in me and that my faith is strong and alive! Your Word determines my opinions, judgments and responses. I am not controlled by my natural senses because my life is the daily expression of Your Word. Hallelujah! Precious Lord Jesus, I love and worship You. You have given me an incorruptible inheritance and a glorious life in You and I am eternally grateful to You! In You I have found everything: life, power, joy, wealth, satisfaction, peace, and security. It is my desire to know and love You more every day. I desire Your constantly manifested presence in me and with me every moment of my life here on earth and forever. I cannot do anything with eternal value without Your Spirit who manifests Your presence to me. Thank You Lord, I live perpetually in Your manifested presence. These are my faith declarations and they are established unto me in Jesus' Name. The light of God's favor shines upon my ways! Hallelujah!

Day 5

I DECLARE and DECREE that I am grateful for who God is in my life and for what He has done in and for me. He is my Heavenly Father who loves me with an eternal love that is perfect in Christ. I am complete in Him. My sufficiency is of Him. His ability and wisdom are at work in me mightily. I am not taking for granted the

FAITH DECLARATIONS

people, the opportunities and the favor He has blessed me with. I am focused on my Lord and Savior, Jesus Christ; the Author and Finisher of my faith. I am thankful to God for what I have and I am not complaining about what I do not yet have in the physical realm.

I know all things are mine; all I need to do is to download my need that is already met in Christ from my heavenly reservoir. *"For blessed be the God and Father of our Lord Jesus Christ, who hath blessed us with all spiritual blessings in heavenly places in Christ: According as he hath chosen us in him before the foundation of the world, that we should be holy and without blame before him in love. Having predestinated us unto the adoption of children by Jesus Christ to himself, according to the good pleasure of his will, To the praise of the glory of his grace, wherein he hath made us accepted in the beloved"* (Ephesians 1:3-6).

I see each day as a gift from God. My heart overflows with praise and gratitude for all of His goodness. I am grateful to God for the opportunity to experience each day of my life on earth in His manifested presence where there is fullness of joy and pleasures forever more at His right hand. The Good News that I believe and know today is that because of Jesus' finished work, God is pouring out His blessings upon my life. He is soaking every part of my life with His goodness. Because of Jesus, every blessing is mine and I am living under open heavens. My home, my family, my relationships, my finances, the big things, the little things, my coming in and my going out are all soaked in the favor, health and provision of Jesus Christ my Lord. My position in Christ qualifies me for the blessings of heaven and I cannot get away from God's goodness and mercy because they are my constant companions. By Jesus' finished work, God's grace has won in my life! Hallelujah!

The heavens are open to me and every blessing is mine today because I am seated with Christ. Like the song writer wrote, I sing today: *"How precious did Grace appear, the hour I first believed. My chains are gone. My God, my Savior has ransomed me; And like a flood His mercy rains, Unending love, Amazing grace."* This is my testimony of God. I am who God says I am. I have what God says I have. I can do what God says I can do. God says I am His child and His heir and a joint heir with Christ. Romans 8:16-17. He says all things are mine. 1 Corinthians 3:21. He says I can do all things because of the anointing, Christ, which strengthens me, and because He is the One in me who works in me, both to will and to work for His good pleasure. Philippians 4:13, 2:13. These are my faith declarations and they are established unto me in Jesus' Name. The light of God's favor shines upon my ways. Hallelujah!

Day 6

I DECLARE and DECREE a legacy of faith over my life. I declare that I am storing up blessings for future generations and that my life is marked by excellence and integrity. Because I am making right choices and taking steps of faith by the help of God's Spirit who indwells in me, others are following me. God's abundance surrounds my life today. My life's challenge is to live in a way that will enable others to win; every time I resist temptation, I am winning for my children as well as every time that I am kind and respectful. Every time I help someone in need, help someone to come to church, to come to Christ, to serve and to give, I am storing up mercy for my children, grandchildren and for others in my lineage so that they too can experience God's goodness in years to come. Christ is alive in me!

My life is the manifestation of divinity because I am a partaker of God's divine nature. My body is the tabernacle of the Holy Spirit and I show forth the glory, beauty, excellence and perfections of Christ today. I have the Kingdom of God, peace, joy and the righteousness in the Holy Ghost in me. In the Name of Jesus, I bring forth prosperity, divine health and divine strength. Hallelujah to my Lord Jesus Christ! Father, I thank You that because of Your grace, I am enjoying the glorious liberty of the sons of God today. I have dominion over Satan and the cohorts of darkness; glory to Your Name, Daddy.

I thank You Father that the full package of salvation in Christ Jesus my Lord is mine and I am enjoying every bit of it. Eternal life, wholeness, preservation, divine health, peace, deliverance, safety, security, victory, success, joy, the indwelling of the Holy Spirit, Your manifested presence, the gifts of the Holy Spirit, the fruit of my recreated human spirit and supernatural prosperity are now mine because I am Your heir and a joint- heir with Christ Jesus, my Lord. Lord, You are my bread provider, provision, protection and protector. You are my caretaker; the One who has responsibility over my life forever.

Lord, I have laid all my burdens at Your feet because I have chosen the stress free life. Father, with a heart full of thanksgiving and praise, I worship Your Holy Name; You're exalted above the heavens and Your glory is upon all the earth! There is none like You for Your Kingdom and reign are everlasting! Glory, honor and praise are Yours now and evermore in Jesus' Name. Thank You Father for taking charge of my life; I declare that by the power of Your Spirit working in me, I am effective and fruitful in every good work today. I am bearing fruits unto righteousness in Jesus' Name! My faith is alive and strong, prevailing over circumstances. I refuse to stagger at the Word of God through unbelief; convinced that God's Word never fails, and confident that I have whatsoever I desire when I pray and declare God's Word, in Jesus' Name. Amen. These are my faith declarations and they are established unto me in Jesus' Name. The light of God's favor shines upon my ways. Hallelujah!

Day 7

I AGREE, DECREE and DECLARE that because I am in Christ and I am Christ's, the world belongs to me. I am in agreement and in fellowship with the only True Monarch of the Universe. I am one with Him because I have received His life! Now, I have His character and I partake of His divinity; His nature of righteousness has been imparted to me. I am a sharer of His life and the beneficiary as well as the effulgence (brightness) of His glory. My spirit has been recreated by God and I have ceased to be an ordinary person. I am supernatural and God talks in and through me now. He looks through my eyes and my spirit has been infused with the presence of God; I am no longer ordinary.

God has a great plan for my life and He directs my steps by His Spirit who lives in me. Although I may not always understand how, I know that whatever challenges I may face in my life and ministry do not come as surprises to God, my Father. He is working out every detail of my circumstances to my advantage. Daddy God, thank You that in Your perfect timing, everything is turning out right for me and everyone in my lineage. Father, this is my testimony of Your love and power in my life in Christ. I rejoice in my salvation in Christ Jesus and because of His grace and finished work, my story ends in victory! My final chapter concludes in my fulfilling the destiny that You have given me. No matter what happens, I know Christ is in me and that my end will be glorious.

My life is upwards and forwards forever. There is no backwardness or stagnation in my life and in the work that God has given me to do. Father, I thank You for setting eternity in my heart in such a way that there is no limit to what I can do and influence. Right now, I declare that Your Word is prevailing and taking center stage in my world, in my country, in my state, in my city, in my street, in my family, in my church and in my life. By Your Holy Spirit who lives in me, I declare that men and women are being delivered from darkness and translated into the glorious liberty of Your sons, through the blood of Jesus, in Jesus' Name. I know that the life You have given to me is a victorious and glorious life in Christ and I am living this life now through Your Spirit who lives in me. My Heavenly Father, thank You for taking delight in me and for taking pleasure in my prosperity in every way.

You are able to take the blessings of a thousand years and make it happen in my life in an instance and I declare that you have done it for me now. Therefore, Your favor is abundantly on my life. It is my season of favor, and I am enjoying favor on every side. Praise God! Blessed Father, I thank You for Your wisdom in my heart and in my mouth today! Thank You for the power and impact of Your Word in my life as I speak it forth and chart my course in the direction of my destiny in Jesus' name. I recognize that I am born after the image of the resurrected Christ, having His life and nature in my spirit. I manifest Your life that is in me to my world daily, in Jesus' Name! Amen. These are my faith declarations and they are established unto me in Jesus' Name. The light of God's favor shines upon my ways. Hallelujah!

Day 8

I DECREE and DECLARE that I am in fellowship and communion with the Creator of the Universe. This takes the limits off what I can achieve and how far I can go on the highway of success. I am an heir of all things and God's dream for my life has come to pass; I am God's dream fulfilled in Christ. I was raised together with Christ and His life is in me. I am born of God so I am a world overcomer and Christ in me is the hope of glory. Christ in me is the hope of restoration, the hope of victory and the hope of success. I cannot be stopped by people, disappointments or adversities. God has the solutions to every problem that I will ever face already lined up. Therefore, the right people and the right breaks are in my life now.

I am fulfilling my God-given destiny in Christ. God knows how to make it all work out for my good because He called and chose me for His purpose. I love God and He is in complete control of my life by His Spirit who lives in me. This is why I can live a life of rest and peace in Him. God knows the end from the beginning and He knows my needs. He has met them in Christ; hallelujah! He has already taken care of me! He gave me the mind of Christ; a mind that is renewed daily by His Word. I am filled with the thoughts of God and I reveal the victorious life in Christ everywhere I go. God said that *"I can do all things;"* therefore, I decree and declare that I can do all things.

I am discovering the favor that already belongs to me in Christ and I am sanctified from evil. As a result, there are no mishaps or destruction in my path. In my path are life, peace, victory success, and prosperity. As I go out today, the land is subdued before me and I dwell in safety. Father, I thank You in the Name of the Lord Jesus for the blessing of the Holy Spirit. I receive that blessing today through Your Word in my life and I proclaim the Word in faith. My mind is renewed and my life is transformed by the inherent power of the Word. I am growing in grace and increasing in wisdom. Circumstances are turning around for my good in Jesus' Name. I am walking in the reality of my divine inheritance in Christ because the Word is at work in me. I am not just a hearer of the Word, therefore, my faith is producing results.

The wisdom, knowledge and ability of the Spirit are showing forth through me. My faith is alive and strong and it is prevailing over evil circumstances. I refuse to stagger at the Word of God through unbelief so, I am strong in faith; convinced that God's Word never fails and I am confident that I have whatsoever I desire when I pray in Jesus' Name. Amen! My trust is in the Lamb of God who was burnt by God's fiery judgment meant for me, I go forth daily, neither poor nor feeble, but abundantly supplied, divinely protected and strengthened in Christ. I worship You Lord Jesus. I gratefully submit to You and perpetually yield my rights to You. I reverently defer to You, purposefully align my agenda to Yours, and intentionally live the way You want me to live, because You are the first and last of my life; the Alpha and Omega and I am in You and You are in me. These are my faith declarations and they are established unto me in Jesus' Name. The light of God's favor shines upon my ways. Hallelujah!

Day 9

I TRUST IN THE LORD WITH ALL MY HEART AND I LEAN NOT UNTO MY OWN UNDERSTANDING. THEREFORE, I DECREE and DECLARE that unexpected blessings are coming my way. I have moved forward from barely making it into great abundance in every area of my life and ministry. In all my ways, I acknowledge You Lord, and I am eternally grateful to You because You direct my path. I am not conformed to this world, but I am continually being transformed by the renewing of my mind so that I may prove what is Your good, acceptable and perfect will for me. I thank You Lord that You perfect all that concerns me; Your mercy O Lord, endures forever. I am moving from glory to glory, from success to success, from faith to faith and from victory to victory.

Thank You Father, for opening supernatural doors of opportunities and gates of nations for me that no one can close. You have spoken to the right people about me so, Ephesians 3:20 is a reality in my life and ministry. I am seeing exceedingly, abundantly, above-and-beyond favor and increase in my life and ministry. Thank You Daddy for the amazing things You are doing in my life now. You reward those who seek after You so, my payday is now. It is my set time to be favored and I thank You Father because You are now releasing that moment of favor that You already have in my future. According to **Psalm 68:19**, You daily load our lives with benefits so I am receiving everything You are loading into my life—*"Blessed be the Lord, who daily loadeth us with benefits, even the God of our salvation. Selah."*

My precious Heavenly Father, I thank You because my spirit is sensitive and energized to hear Your voice and receive Your divine counsel, signals, and guidance today. Father, I thank You that You have sent the Holy Spirit to teach me all things and to bring all things that You have said to my remembrance. I rejoice because it is given unto me to understand Your voice in my spirit. Thank You Lord for the wisdom You have given me. The eyes of my mind and spirit are enlightened by Your Spirit to see, understand and apprehend spiritual realities. I recognize that I am born after the image of the resurrected Christ and I have His life and nature in my spirit. Daily, I manifest Your life that is in me to my world in Jesus' name! Daddy God, I am grateful to You that I live the extraordinary life of victory, triumph and glory. The power of Your Word has renewed and transformed my spirit, soul and body. I thank You Father for Your love and the indescribable joy of sharing it with others and revealing to them the compassion of Christ in Jesus' Name.

Lord my full attention is on what You are doing right now. I refuse to worry or be worked up about what may or may not happen tomorrow. You are leading my life and Lord; You are able to help me deal with whatever hard things come up when the time comes. These are my faith declarations and they are established unto me. The light of God's favor shines upon my ways. Hallelujah!

Day 10

I DECREE and DECLARE that, because my trust is in God, He has accelerated His plan for my life and I am accomplishing my dreams faster than I thought possible. I am debt free and I am winning people into God's kingdom. I am meeting the right people; excellent things are now happening faster in my life and ministry than before. In Christ Jesus, I am a victor over every challenge. God's blessings in my life are thrusting me years ahead. God is in the accelerating mode in my ministry, in my life, and in my family. His one good break can thrust me thirty years down the road and He knows how to speed up natural laws concerning me. He can take me farther more quickly than I could ever imagine. By the power of the Holy Spirit, I am making progress and I am moving very quickly and fast forward in my life and in my ministry. This is the set time for my advancement, therefore, in the Name of Jesus; I am favored and prosperous in all things. My Lord Jesus Christ came to Planet Earth on a divine mission to make men sons of God and His mission was a huge success; He finished the job completely.

By His finished work, He qualified me to enjoy prosperity in all things and to excel in all my endeavors. I am prospering spiritually, mentally, financially, physically and materially. I am sanctified from evil. Therefore, there are no mishaps or destructions on my path. In my path are life, peace, success, victory and prosperity. As I go out today, the land is subdued before me and I dwell in safety. Father, I thank You for Your anointing upon my life. I am an able minister of the Gospel because You have made me so. I take advantage of Your anointing in and upon my life as well as Your grace and wisdom in me to fulfill the ministry that You have assigned to me in Jesus' Name. The anointing which I have received from You abides in me forever and through it, I am energized for productivity and positioned for effectiveness. I take advantage of that anointing today as I use it to bless my world and do exploits to the praise and glory of Your name.

The Lord has made me to be the head and not tail in all areas of my life and ministry. I am positioned above only and not beneath and I am now first and not last in everything. The Lord has made something beautiful out of my life in Jesus Name and my faith in the Lord is my victory. I have overcome Satan, his cohorts and the systems of this world. I am confident in the power and ability of the Word of God which I believe and by which I move from glory to glory in Jesus' Name; Amen. God's Word builds me up and fills my heart with divine treasures that cause me to bring forth fruits unto righteousness. Father, I yield my heart to Your Spirit who causes me to be productive and effective in every good work. "He leads me. He is not behind me, shouting, Go! He is ahead of me bidding, "Come!"

He is in front, clearing the path, cutting the bush. He is standing next to the rocks. He only warns me, Watch your step there." I completely trust His love, wisdom, ability and guidance. I love You Lord. These are my faith declarations and they are established unto me. The light of Your favor shines upon my ways constantly. Hallelujah!

Day 11

I DECREE and DECLARE **Ephesians 3:20** over my life and over my ministry today. God is doing exceedingly, abundantly above all that I ask or think and that because I honor Him, His blessings are chasing me down and overtaking me. I am always in the right place at the right time. People go out of their way to be good to me because I am clothed with God's favor. God is multiplying my resources for increased giving. As a financier of the Gospel, my capacity to give towards the furtherance of the Gospel increases and because my Heavenly Father makes all grace abound towards me. Therefore, I am self-sufficient in Christ; possessing enough to require no aid or support. I am furnished in abundance for Kingdom expansion by the anointing of the Holy Spirit.

I am living a life of favor; a life of giving and I am working miracles by the power of the Holy Spirit in the Name of Jesus. Like Mary, the mother of the Lord Jesus Christ, I declare, *"My soul doth magnify the Lord, And my spirit hath rejoiced in God my Saviour. For he hath regarded the low estate of his handmaiden: for, behold, from henceforth all generations shall call me blessed. For he that is mighty hath done to me great things; and holy is his name. And his mercy is on them that fear him from generation to generation. He hath shewed strength with his arm; he hath scattered the proud in the imagination of their hearts. He hath put down the mighty from their seats, and exalted them of low degree. He hath filled the hungry with good things; and the rich he hath sent empty away. He hath holpen his servant Israel, in remembrance of his mercy; As he spake to our fathers, to Abraham, and to his seed forever"* (Luke 1:46-55).

I am God's outstretched arm; His expression of help, healing, deliverance and salvation to the world. I am a blessing to my generation and a conveyor of the glory, grace, and excellence of divinity. Blessed be God! I am the fulfillment of God's dream because I am the proof of Christ's righteousness. I am the expression of His love and perfection and Christ is my wisdom. The anointing of Christ has become my wisdom so that I do not lack wisdom; wisdom is working in me. I celebrate wisdom and wisdom has put a crown of glory on my head. Wisdom is my friend and my life is full of peace.

Life and immortality have been unveiled through the Gospel of Christ Jesus, and I am the bearer of this good news in my world. God has anointed me to deliver men from bondage into the glorious liberty of the sons of God through the power of the Gospel; therefore I am passionate about leading others to Christ. Today I manifest the glories, beauty, and power of the life of Christ in me. I am greatly rejoicing in the Lord, my soul is joyful in my God; for He has clothed me in the garments of salvation, He has covered me with the robe of righteousness in Jesus' Name Amen. I am conscious of the robe of righteousness that God has clothed me with. I know that in this robe, I have pockets labeled: favor," "divine health," "divine protection," "divine supply," "divine wisdom," "family blessings," "eternal life," and so much more. These are my faith declarations and they are established unto me. The light of God's favor shines upon my ways. Hallelujah!

Day 12

I DECREE and DECLARE that, I am special and that I am extraordinary. I am wonderfully and beautifully made in the image and likeness of God my Father. Therefore, I am one of a kind. I am God's masterpiece; His most prized possession. I square up my shoulders and I keep my head held up high because I know that I am a child of the Most High God. I am the living tabernacle of divinity and the headquarters of the Godhead. I am God's dream fulfilled and I did not have to sweat or struggle for it. I did not do anything by myself to earn it; the grace of the Lord Jesus Christ conferred it upon me.

I am God's offspring; a progeny of success! God made me in His image and likeness for beauty, success and glory. He already gave the verdict in **Psalm 1:3** that whatsoever I do shall prosper. Therefore, I refuse to struggle in life. Excellence and success are in my spirit. I am born of the Word; therefore, I have overcome the world and its systems of failure and defeat. I have in me the seed of success, greatness and prosperity so, I live victoriously in Christ and I manifest His excellence and glory. I am a chosen generation; which means that I belong to a new generation of supermen with divine genetic materials! I have God's DNA in me. Therefore, I am more than a conqueror.

My lineage is one of champions and victors. As a result, no earthly generational curse, sickness or disease can work against me or destroy me because I am a new creation. I have new genes that came from my Heavenly Father. Because God gave birth to me, I am a success already. I belong to the new race Jesus died and rose again from the dead to produce. Christ is in me now; I have the hope of glory — *"for in Him dwelleth all the fullness of the Godhead bodily"* (Colossians 2:9).

Now that I have Christ, I have everything. Now that I am in Christ, I am home; the journey is over. I am perfected in Him and I am complete in Him. My Heavenly Father is the most important personality in my life and my Lord Jesus is the personality of my deepest affection. The Holy Spirit is my Boss and Friend. He has the final say in all that concerns me and what He says concerning me is what counts. I was not mass produced. I am God's masterpiece — (Ephesians 2:10). God delights in me and I am His inheritance. He rejoices over me with joy and **Zephaniah 3:17** confirms it, *"The LORD thy God in the midst of thee is mighty; he will save, <u>he will rejoice over thee with joy</u>; he will rest in his love, he will joy over thee with singing."*

I am a victor in Christ Jesus! The Greater One lives in me and He is greater than he that is in the world. The Word of faith that changes things is in my heart and mouth today, prevailing over circumstances and situations in the Name of Jesus. Satan and his cohorts are under my feet; and I live perpetually in victory, health, dominion and righteousness, in Jesus' Name. Amen. These are my faith declarations and they are established unto me. The light of God's favor shines upon my ways. Hallelujah!

Day 13

I DECREE and DECLARE that God has brought about new seasons of growth and development in my life, in my family and in my ministry. Father, I thank You for energizing me and everyone in my sphere of contact for victory and success. I am grateful to You Daddy for positioning us for the transcendental life by Your Spirit who lives in us! By Him, I now work according to the working of Your power that works within me mightily. I am now excelling in every area of my life and ministry because the standard of competence and excellence by which I operate is by the Holy Spirit. I therefore, refuse to be stagnant and to hold on to the old. I am now open to change, knowing that God is doing something new in my life, in my family and in my ministry.

He said, *"I will do a new thing."* He is doing it now in this day and hour and I am showing forth His praise. Lord, here is Your Word for me in **Isaiah 43:18-21**, *"Remember ye not the former things, neither consider the things of old. Behold, I will do a new thing; now it shall spring forth; shall ye not know it? I will even make a way in the wilderness, and rivers in the desert. The beast of the field shall honour me, the dragons and the owls: because I give waters in the wilderness, and rivers in the desert, to give drink to my people, my chosen.* **This people have I formed for myself; they shall shew forth my praise.***"*

Lord, I trust You with all my heart. New doors of opportunities and gates of nations are now open to me to reach the unreached and to tell the untold of their need of salvation in Christ Jesus. New relationships and new levels of favor are now mine because it is my set time to experience Your unprecedented favor and that of men. I am enjoying the manifold blessings of God in every area of my life, my family and my ministry. I declare that all things are working together for good for me because I love the Lord and I have been called according to His purpose. Everything that I require for life and godliness has been delivered unto me and I am enjoying life to the full in Jesus' Name!

I am God's dream fulfilled as a result of His grace and His grace alone. I am a chosen generation and I am already a success and a victor. I am the effulgence of God's glory, beauty and grace; I am not and can never be ordinary. I am conscious of the supernatural life of God in me; therefore, greatness, excellence and success are in my spirit! I am functioning from my spirit; therefore, I cannot be subject to any health conditions. Because I function from my spirit, I can never be broke in my life and my business cannot fail.

My finances cannot fail and I cannot be disadvantaged. Nothing about me can fail because I function from my spirit, I have dominion and I walk in dominion. I walk in victory and in prosperity. Lord, I bow my heart before You, as I open my hands and declare, "Lord, It's all You. I am nothing but a vessel unto honor, fit and meet for Your holy use. Lord, use me as You will." These are my faith declarations and they are established unto me. The light of God's favor shines upon my ways. Hallelujah!

Day 14

I DECREE and DECLARE that the words that I speak are spirit and life. They are seasoned with grace and they are full of love and power. They are spoken to bless my hearers. My words always come to pass because they are the very words of God; my Father who lives in me. Right now, I speak favor and victory over the entire family of God on earth, over my immediate family, over my friends and over all my loved ones. I am proud of them and I love them all. They are amazing, talented and they are the beautiful people of the beloved country of God. They are doing great things in life.

My words carry God's supernatural power and they release favor, ability, confidence and God's goodness in extraordinary ways. This is because Jesus Christ is such a delight to God the Father and He satisfies God's heart completely; what He did, He did for me. God is satisfied with me because Jesus satisfied Him for me. Jesus is God's delight so, I am God's delight and because He pleases God, I please God too. Because Jesus is my righteousness and perfection, I stand righteous and perfect before God.

I thank You Daddy that I can do all things through Christ which strengthens me. I thank You Lord Jesus for Your grace that has brought me acceptability, favor, joy, peace, happiness, love and great advantage! Lord, at the cross, You gave Yourself completely and You made provisions for the forgiveness of my sins that no one else could. You chose to lay down Your life in exchange for mine and as a result, all my sins, failures and mistakes are forever washed away by the precious blood You shed on my behalf at Calvary! Truly, in

Christ we have redemption through His blood; the forgiveness of sins *"according to the riches of His grace."*

Today, I walk in total well-being and good success because I have accepted my Lord Jesus as my Commander in chief and I follow His revelations to me every day. God is the One who is working in me to will and to do of His good pleasure. I follow Him daily and He has made me a fisher of men. His Spirit lives in me and by Him, I am winning people to Christ. As my Commander in chief, He does not allow anything to happen in my life except He has a purpose for it. Nothing happens to me; but all things happen for me.

All things are working together for my good because Jesus, the God of the Universe is calling the shots in my life. Lord, I go into this day knowing that You are for me and in me by Your Spirit. Therefore, I am a victor on every side and my life is heavily <u>graced</u>. I am growing in that grace wherein I stand daily and I am also growing in the knowledge of You, my Lord and Savior Jesus Christ. My life is flooded through and through with joy and gladness. Indeed You have prepared a table of delights, a feast of all good things for me. My heart is merry and I have a continual feast. Indeed my cup runs over and surely goodness and mercy are my constant companions all the days of my life, as I dwell in the house of the Lord forever. These are my faith declarations and they are established unto me. The light of God's favor shines upon my ways. Hallelujah!

Day 15

I DECREE and DECLARE that I have a sound mind that is filled with God's thoughts. By my faith in the finished work of Christ Jesus my Lord, I am well able. I function with divine wisdom and my ability is of God. My sufficiency is of God because I am complete in Him. He is my life and strength and I am anointed by Him. I am well equipped by His Spirit and grace to rule and reign in life; I am favored! I am empowered and every day, my thoughts are guided by the Word of God. The Word of God has programmed my life for success so, I am unstoppable and I am indestructible. I know who I am; I am a success and a victor in Christ.

I am grateful to God, my Father that my Lord Jesus is my burnt offering. All that Jesus is before God I am also because of His grace.

Jesus is God's righteousness and so am I. He is the perfect expression of God's excellence, beauty and perfection and so am I in Him. I am an heir of God and a joint-heir with Christ. He has unclouded favor with God; therefore, I have and I enjoy unclouded favor with God as well. As The Lord Jesus is before the Father, so am I. I have the mind of Christ and I am full of His resurrection power. God and I are a majority so I cannot be defeated. There are more for me than are against me and I am equipped and anointed. I see myself as God sees me; a victor in Christ. Satan is very scared of me because the Greater One dwells in me. I am glowing with God's glory and God's hedge of protection is all over me and over everyone in my lineage.

I have nothing to fear because my Lord Jesus has already cleared my path of any evil by His finished work. I have come into agreement with Him and my life is more fulfilling and more rewarding now. Dear Heavenly Father, I thank You for making me the dispenser of Your blessings and Your goodness to my world. Thank You that I am the extension and the manifestation of Your grace, love and compassion to all those that I come in contact with daily because You have made me an able minister of the Gospel (not of the letter but of the Spirit) that gives life in Jesus' Name; Amen.

Father, I thank You that I am walking in prosperity. Daily, I am revealing to my world through my words and actions the glory, virtues and perfections of Your divinity that You deposited into my spirit! My dear heavenly Father, You have chosen me from the foundation of the world to reveal Christ in me. I fix my gaze on You and Your eternal grace, holding forth the Word of life and truth, as I bear fruits unto righteousness to Your praise and glory, in Jesus Name. Amen.

Father, I thank You that my life is for Your glory. Your perfect will is established in my life and in the lives of everyone in my lineage and sphere of contact today, Daddy. Hallelujah! Glory to Your holy Name! These are my conscious faith declarations and they are established unto me. The light of Your favor shines upon my ways continually. Hallelujah! I love You Daddy God.

Day 16

I DECREE and DECLARE that in the Name of Jesus, I am working miracles, I am healing the sick and I am setting the captives free. I am sensitive to the needs of those around me and through the Spirit of God who lives in me, I am getting their needs met. The fallen are lifted by the power of God that is working through me and the broken are getting restored. I am full of compassion and kindness; as a result, I encourage the discouraged. I am a miracle worker that is showing God's love and mercy everywhere I go.

As Jesus is, so am I in this world; I am like Jesus! I am a container filled with God and I am God's masterpiece! This is my mind set and I dispense the goodness of God everywhere I go. The light of God's favor shines upon my ways. As a matter of fact, because I am in union with Christ Jesus my Lord, God's favor is flooding my life and my ministry right now through His Spirit who dwells in me. Thank You Father that all that You said belongs to me in **1 John 5:11-13** are mine — *"And this is the record that God hath given to us eternal life, and this life is in his Son. He that hath the Son hath life; and he that hath not the Son of God hath not life. These things have I written unto You that believe on the name of the Son of God; that ye may know that ye have eternal life, and that ye may believe on the name of the Son of God."*

I believe on the name of the Son of God; therefore, I have the Son and I have eternal life. All the blessings that come with eternal life are mine in Christ. I am as valuable to God as Jesus is. The Lord Jesus, the Son of the Living God is the price that God paid to bring me into His divine royal family and the Lord Jesus gave me the glory the Father gave Him. God's provisions and blessings are abundant in my life. God's blessings crown my head according **Proverbs 10:6**, glory to God! His bountiful provisions are upon me and upon my entire family. We have arrived in the place of abundance, where we enjoy unlimited wealth and divine health. We are making progress and moving forward in all we do. We have been brought into a large place and we can do all that God said that we can do! God loves us as He loves Jesus.

We are all blessings going somewhere to happen. We are called by the Name of the Lord; wherever we go, we are blessed and we are a blessing. The people around us look at us favorably because they know that we are bundles of blessings going somewhere to happen! The Lord is in us and for us. We are mightily helped of God and we are excited about it. God is the One in charge of our lives and we trust Him completely. He does not allow anything to happen in our lives, except He has a purpose for it. Whatever happens in our lives does not happen to us (for evil) but happens for us (for good). God ordained all things to work together for our good. Lord we recognize Your dealings with us, Eternal Life flows through our beings in all Its sanctifying, invigorating and remedial force. We know, are aware of You, as the only true God, and our Lord Jesus Christ, Your Son. These are my faith declarations and they are established unto me. The light of God's favor shines upon my ways. Hallelujah! Thank You Daddy!

Day 17

I DECREE and DECLARE that my faith in God is proven by my submission to God's Word and His Spirit who are working the works of God in and through my life. I am a vessel unto honor fit and meet for the Master's use. He recreated me in righteousness and true holiness like Himself, and set me apart for His glory and holy use. The Spirit of God who raised Jesus from the dead lives in me. I have the power of attorney to use the Name of Jesus. When I call on that wonderful and powerful Name, every knee bows, and every tongue confesses that Jesus is Lord to the glory of God, the Father. I have the grace advantage all the time. Therefore, I am able to attempt great things for God by faith in His Word through the Holy Spirit and I am getting tremendous results.

His grace is multiplied abundantly in my life and ministry. I know my God and I am doing exploits in the awesome Name of Jesus by the power of the Holy Ghost. I am not just praying prayers or just believing, I am putting my faith to work by attempting great things for God's glory. I follow God's initiatives and He completes what He has started through me. I am fruitful in every good work. I am the expression of His righteousness and power. The culture of the Gospel of Christ is expressed through me. I am the expression of His righteousness, glory and power. My life is an unending stream of God's glory. My life is imbued with the miracle-working power of God. I am an associate of the God-kind and a participator of the divine nature. God has brought me into union with Himself.

I am a participant of the divine experience. I am a miracle distributor because the miracle-worker Himself lives in me. The Holy Spirit has made me indomitable and brought excellence into my life. The Word of God in my mouth is my victory over adversities and the challenges of life. I declare in the Name of Jesus that I am blessed forever. I am prosperous and highly favored. I declare that it is impossible for me to be sick, broke or afflicted. God's Word testifies of me that I am the righteousness of God. That I am born of God and I am an overcomer. My destiny is shaped by God' perfect will for me in Jesus' Name!

I am conscious of the Christ in me! I am filled with the knowledge of God's will and I am fruitful in all I do. The Lord has made me a master in everything. **2 Corinthians 3:5** tells me that my competence is of God and with the knowledge of His will, I am competent. It does not matter where I am; I am fruitful in every good work. It is the Almighty God who has empowered me and I am full of the Holy Ghost. I function in the dominion of the Spirit daily, conscious that all things are mine, in the name of Jesus. Amen.

I deal wisely in all my affairs today, in Jesus' Name. Amen. These are my faith declarations and they are established unto me. The light of God's favor shines upon my ways. Hallelujah!

Day 18

I DECREE and DECLARE that because I am born of God, sudden flow of God's favor are flooding my life and His mighty power is mightily at work in and through me. God is overwhelming me and amazing me with His favor in this Season of Favor. My children are mighty in the land and they are serving God with their lives through the Holy Spirit. They are God's glory and are living for His glory. My life is filled with God's peace, power, purpose and plenty. Jesus is my salvation, my life, my peace, my healing, my wisdom and my provision, my all —He is my all in all! He is my "I AM" who has fought my battles and has given me the victory. He is my soon coming King and He is the High Priest of my confessions who makes good every word I speak. According to **Isaiah 26:3**, God is keeping me in perfect peace because my mind stays on Him and my confident trust is in Him. Wisdom is the Word of God and Christ is made unto me Wisdom according to **1 Corinthians 1:30**.

I dwell in perfect peace, perfect prosperity and perfect health. I choose the right thoughts and I do the right things the first time because Jesus is my wisdom. I am the fulfillment of God's dream and the proof of Christ's righteousness. I am the expression of His love and perfection. I am not speaking so that these things <u>will be</u> because <u>they are already true</u> in the spiritual realm. Therefore, I am downloading into my physical reality on earth, what belongs to me in Christ so that it will be for me on earth as it is in heaven. God has blessed me with all spiritual blessings in the heavenly places in Christ and because I am in the physical realm, I bring them to my realm where I can enjoy them. My faith in God is my power to do this.

Thank You my precious Heavenly Father for the awesome privilege and blessing of having the Holy Spirit live in me and for His enabling me to do this in Jesus Name. Thank You Daddy, because today, my spirit is sensitive and energized to hear Your voice and to receive divine counsel, signals and guidance. I rejoice because it is given unto me to understand Your Word and to hear Your voice in my spirit! I thank You Father for the influence of your Word in my life, in my family and in my ministry in Jesus' Name.

I take my stand in my place in Christ and I am focused on the Word of God. The more I give attention to God's Word, the more it is having power and influence in my life. By the help of the Holy Spirit, I am getting a hold of God's Word; knowing it and getting the Word revealed through me. My knowledge of the Word has positioned me not just to know about the existence of the Godhead, but to become aware of the only true God, my Lord Jesus Christ and my Father, the Holy Spirit who indwells in me. As I have become aware of the Godhead, all for whom I care are linked to God, too. As I yield my service to God, I draw, by the magnetic power of Love, in my loved ones within the Divine-Life radius. These are my faith declarations and they are established unto me. The light of God's favor shines upon my ways. Hallelujah!

Day 19

I BELIEVE, DECIDE, AGREE, AND DECREE that there is an anointing of ease on my life so that I can take delight in God and joyfully look unto Him. He has made the crooked places straight before me because I am yoked to The Lord Jesus Christ; His yoke is easy and His burden is light. I am in Him and He is in me! Therefore, I stand in His grace and I operate from a position of rest because of His finished work. Goodness and mercy are my constant companions everywhere I go. God is directing every step I take by His Spirit. By the power of God's Spirit, I am clothed with the full armor of God and my mind and imagination are protected with the helmet of salvation. My thoughts are focused steadfastly on God's love and power. Christ's righteousness is my breastplate that is protecting my heart and emotions so that I will not be governed by my feelings. My spirit is wrapped with God's belt of truth that is protecting me from deception.

My steps are girded with the sandals of peace and my feet are set firmly in the Good News of God's salvation and love for the world. God by His Spirit has empowered me to stand firm against any demonic attack. My shield of faith is protecting me from Satan's arrows as I stand shoulder to shoulder with God's army in opposition against his schemes. I fight the good fight of faith and I operate by the sword of the Spirit which is the Word of God that is planted deep in my heart in a fresh and exciting way. Therefore, I am always ready to deflect and cut down lies with God's truth and I pray always with all prayer and supplication in the Spirit while watching thereunto with all perseverance and supplication for all saints. I proclaim my victory today! The Holy Spirit has a ministry in my life and He is the One leading me always. He does it from my inner man and He leads me from glory to glory. He shows me what could be better than my now and He is making my life much more glorious every day.

I am shining because He told me to *"arise and shine."* Because I am shining, Gentiles are coming to my light and Kings are coming to the brightness of my rising. God has sent me to reassign desolate heritages. The world belongs to God and He has sent me to establish the Kingdom of heaven in the hearts of men. God is working through His Spirit in me and I am in full cooperation. The Kingdom of God is expanding through my ministry and I am sponsoring the Gospel of Christ big time. I am doing great things with and for God and I live in an atmosphere of joy, peace, and prosperity. I am excellent all the way and I do excellent things. That is who I am by the Spirit of God and I am a light to the nations. I am wise with the wisdom of God. Lord, I bless and praise You, for Your blessings in our lives. Yours, O Lord, is the greatness, The power and the glory, The victory and the majesty; For all that is in heaven and in earth is Yours; Yours is the Kingdom, O Lord. And You are exalted as head over all. In Your hand is power and might; In Your hand it is to make great And to give strength to all. Now therefore our God, We thank You And praise Your glorious Name. Amen. 1Chronicles 29:11-13. These are my faith declarations. They are my mind set; the mindset of the righteous and they are established for me. God's favor shines upon my ways. Hallelujah!

Day 20

I DECIDE, AGREE, AND DECREE that I am cool, calculated and calm. Nothing can steal my joy which is a fruit of my recreated spirit in Christ. I am above only and I am never beneath any circumstance. I am an OVERCOMER all the time and I am not of this world; therefore, I am not subject to the circumstances and rudiments of this earthly realm. Christ Jesus gave me eternal life –the overcoming, indestructible, unconquerable life of God and I walk with this consciousness daily. Glory is to God who has given me the power to always be cool and collected; and has assured me of His love for me which He proved at Calvary cross; where He gave me His best by the sacrifice of His Son in my place. He told me that He will never leave me and that He will not forsake me. He showed me that He is my "I AM;" ever present with and in me. He is all I will ever need.

He told me that I am His very own so, I am grateful and excited that I belong to Jesus Christ. He is there for me no matter the challenges that I may face; for the battle is the Lord's. I have chosen to live a joyous and peaceful life in Him because He gave me the victory and made me a victor in Himself; I can never be a victim. In the Name of Jesus, I have set in motion the forces of life to attract unto me the men and women, the circumstances, the finances, the divine grace and favor that align with the call of God for my life and ministry. This is what is happening in my life and ministry right now by the power of the Holy Spirit; therefore, I am calm and I am never in haste about anything because I know whom I believe. He is faithful and He will never fail me. He is never late and His timing and choices are always the best. He showed me this in His infallible Word and it is so in my life.

When something is happening to me, I know that He is doing something in me; something that will shape me for eternity. The only things that matter in my life are eternal things. <u>I know through His Word and from the Holy Spirit that the secret of a successful life in God's Kingdom is to keep my focus on eternal things. I also know that there is more to life than material comforts and sensual experiences</u>. By the help of the Holy Spirit, I am mixing prayer with worship and I am heavenly focused. Father, I worship you and give you thanks for giving me wisdom and revelation in the knowledge of Jesus Christ my Lord. For to know Jesus is to have grace and peace multiplied unto me. To know Jesus is to receive all things pertaining to life and godliness. Thank You Daddy that my faith is in Jesus' victory. I have overcome Satan, all his cohorts and the systems of this world.

I am confident in the power and ability of the Word of God which I have believed and by which I live. I use it to move from grace to grace, from victory to victory, from success to success, from prosperity to prosperity, and from glory to glory; this is my life in Christ. These are my faith declarations and they are established unto me. The light of God's favor shines upon my ways continually. Hallelujah!

Day 21

I AGREE, DECREE, AND DECLARE that God's supernatural favor is functioning in my life, in my ministry, in my family, and in my sphere of influence. I am a success happening in my world through the Holy Spirit. Supernatural opportunities, restoration and divine favor are coming my way. I am getting stronger, healthier, younger, and wiser with the wisdom of God. By the ministry of the Holy Spirit <u>in and through</u> my life, I am discovering talent that I did not know I had. I am accomplishing my God-given dreams and God has arranged all things in my favor. He has lined up the right people and the right opportunities for me. I am experiencing supernatural increase in my ministry and in my family. God's explosive and multiplied blessings are abundant in my life, in my ministry and in my family. By the unction of the Holy Spirit, abundance is present in my life and I am preaching the Gospel of Jesus Christ every time and everywhere. *For, I am not ashamed of the Gospel of Christ because it is the power of God unto salvation.*

I represent Him through the Holy Spirit everywhere I go. He is in me and I am eternally secured in God's love. God has placed my life in Christ who is the All-deserving One. I have become all-deserving because Jesus qualified me and gave me a blood-bought right to every blessing of God. I have a blood-bought right to a life full of meaning, purpose and abundance. I have a blood-bought right to walk in divine favor, divine abundance, divine protection, and divine health. I have a blood-bought right to all of God's provisions; even in a depressed economy. I have a blood-bought competitive advantage and preferential treatment because God favors me. I have a blood-bought right to the excellent life in Christ. My dear Heavenly Father, I thank you for the life of Christ in me. I accept and affirm the truth of who I am in Christ who is my wholeness and who also, has been made unto me righteousness, wisdom and sanctification.

In the Name of the Lord Jesus, my whole life is an epitome of excellence and God's beauty; Amen. God is my Supplier and all my needs are met according to his riches in glory by Christ Jesus who rules the universe from His throne on high. He is watching me and I do what the Holy Spirit reveals to me to do. The fire of God is in my bones and the anointing is on the increase, incorruptibly, in my life. I operate by this anointing and I do not rely on my strength at all. God's ability is my ability because the Holy Spirit has baptized me into Christ. He is inside me and He empowers me to do the works of God. God is God and I will do what He sent me to do. I am bold because I know who I am; I am not just "a talker of the Word" but "a doer of the Word" because I am the Word. I live the Word. I am not a forgetful hearer of the Word of God. I hear to do and I am blessed in my deeds. By the power of the Holy Spirit I have been brought into oneness with God. I refuse to be separated from this Union with divinity, by anything the world, the devil, and the flesh may be offering. I am completely grateful and sold out to God; because of His mercy and grace in my life. DADDY GOD, I AM YOURS FOREVER IN CHRIST JESUS, MY LORD. These are my declarations and they are established unto me. The light of God's favor is shining upon my ways. Hallelujah!

Day 22

I DECREE AND AGREE WITH GOD'S SPIRIT that I was created in the image and likeness of God (to look like Him) and to function as He does. As Jesus is righteous, so am I in Him. He is victorious, so am I in Him and I have the DNA of God. I am clothed with divine favor and I am royalty. I have the royal blood of divinity flowing in my veins and I am the head and not tail; above only and never beneath. I am moving forwards and I am making progress! I live with purpose, passion, praise and with the expectation of the Lord's return. I am a winner in Christ and I boldly declare in the Name of Jesus that I am highly favored of God and men. I am favored in the city and in the country. All situations and circumstances around me align for my good in Jesus' Name. I belong to God's chosen generation. I am a royal priest, a holy person and a peculiar being in the class of God.

God has called me out of darkness into His marvelous light to show forth His praises. I am God's offspring and a progeny of success. God made me in His image and likeness for beauty, glory and success. He already gave the verdict in **Psalm 1:3** that whatsoever I do shall prosper. Therefore, I refuse to struggle in life because excellence and success are in my spirit! I am indestructible and unstoppable because I am born of the Word of God. In Christ, I have overcome the world and its systems of failure and defeat. I have in me the seed of success, greatness and prosperity. I live victoriously in Christ; manifesting His excellent presence and glory.

The LORD has shown me the path of life and He is my life. In His presence is fullness of joy and at His right hand are pleasures forever more —**Psalm 16:11**. Hallelujah! Lord, this is the day that

You have made; the day that You have given me as a gift to rejoice in and be glad in. Thank You Lord for helping me to remember that there is nothing in this day that You and I cannot handle together. Daddy, I thank You for empowering me with supernatural ability to do the impossible and also to effect changes in my world. Today, I take full advantage of my authority in Christ and I declare peace, prosperity, progress and increase for me, my loved ones, all in my world, and in my country.

I praise You Lord and I give my day to You Father because You are in charge of my life. I worship and yield to Your Spirit in Jesus' Name. My life is the expression of Your glory. Christ is exalted in me and His divinity is manifested through me today as I live to fulfill His purpose and to do His perfect will! Thank You Father for Your wisdom, ability and power those are inherent in me; in Jesus' Name. Amen. I thank You Father for Your passionate love for me. Two thousand years ago, in the person of Your Son, You put on skin, came to Earth, and gave Your very life to atone for my sin and prove Your deep love for me. You paid the ultimate price to reconcile me to Yourself, it goes to show how much You love, value and want me. You don't need me to be who You are- GOD, but You love me affectionately because, You made me in Your image and likeness. O! How I appreciate Your love for me Daddy God! These are my declarations and they are established unto me. God's favor is shining upon my ways. Hallelujah!

Day 23

I DECREE and AGREE that I am an offspring of the Word of God; therefore, I live in and by the Word. I have peace with God through faith. Thus, I am experiencing a day-to-day transformation and renewal by the Holy Spirit. I am stirred and positioned for greatness, effectiveness and excellence; I walk in the victory of Christ every day of my life. God made me to live in me and in oneness with me; He is in me for a purpose. God lives in me to reveal His glory to the nations of the world and I agree and declare this so; it is the reality in my life. I am a world changer and anyone in my sphere of influence is blessed and graced. As Jesus is, so am I in this world. I am marked by God's love; I am the focus of His delight.

The gracious hand of God is upon my life forever. Hallelujah to my Lord Jesus Christ; my righteousness forever.

As the Holy Spirit recorded in **Ephesians 2:4-10**, I am now in the class of God; seated with Christ Jesus because He is rich in mercy towards me —*"But God, who is rich in mercy, for his great love wherewith he loved us, Even when we were dead in sins, hath quickened us together with Christ, (by grace ye are saved;)* **<u>And hath raised us up together, and made us sit together in heavenly places in Christ Jesus:</u>** <u>*That in the ages to come he might shew the exceeding riches of his grace in his kindness toward us through Christ Jesus*</u>. *For by grace are ye saved through faith; and that not of yourselves: it is the gift of God: Not of works, lest any man should boast. For we are his workmanship, created in Christ Jesus unto good works, which God hath before ordained that we should walk in them."*

I am who God says that I am. God has deposited seeds of greatness in my spirit and I have the mentality of the seed of greatness. I am blessed and talented; I have been handpicked by the God of the universe. I am a history maker and I am destined to leave a mark on this generation. I am blessed and I am a blessing to my world. I know where I am going and I am getting there by reprogramming my life with what God has said to me. I am unstoppable because I have my Heavenly Father's approval. His Spirit, my Helper lives in me and is helping me all the way and all the time. He is taking me to places that I could never go on my own.

I am all God says I am and I do not care what anybody says; I believe and agree with what God has said about me. I am blessed, equipped and anointed to accomplish my divine destiny. I am a saint of God; a saint of great grace, great faith, great significance, great courage, great fortune and great talent in Christ. I am a champion in Christ. There is a King in me and the Lord Jesus is His NAME—He made me a king! As a result, I am royalty and I have my robe of honor on, because of His finished work- The Son of Man was flayed to the bone to the extent that He no longer resembled a human being. And that torture was followed by something even worse, the crucifixion itself, the vilest method of execution ever devised. As Jesus hung on the cross for me, His Father in heaven "turned away" from Him. Habakkuk 1:13 confirms that God's eyes "are too pure to look on evil." He was forsaken of God that I can be accepted. On the cross Christ cried out: My God, my God, why have you forsaken me? (Matthew 27:46).

This is the price God paid for me, and this is how I know who I am and that God truly loves me. Because of this incredible and unwarranted love for me a disobedient sinner, I am offered eternal life, God's nature of righteousness, abundant grace, salvation, and a place in Him forever. I have accepted my full package of salvation in Christ Jesus and I am reigning and ruling in life by Him. God has shown His love for me in that while I was still a sinner, Christ died for me. Since, therefore I have been justified by His blood, much more shall I be saved by Him from the wrath of God.

For if while I was an enemy I was reconciled to God by the death of His Son, much more, now that I am reconciled, shall I be saved by His life. More than that, I also rejoice in God through our Lord Jesus Christ, through whom I have now received reconciliation. Romans 5: 8-11. These are my faith declarations and they are established unto me. The light of God's favor shines upon my ways continually.

Day 24

I DECREE and AGREE that I am a new creation in Christ Jesus; therefore, I walk in the glorious liberty of the sons of God. I am freely enjoying my inheritance in Christ. I have been made free from sin, sickness, bondage and the second death by the law of the Spirit of life in Christ Jesus. Hallelujah! I am strong and I am full of energy because God is my life and strength. He has exalted me and I am in His class of beings. He made me in His image and likeness to look like Him and to function like Him. I am blessed, strong, talented and creative just as He is. I am having a productive day today; glory be to God!

Lord, I thank You for helping me to remember that there is nothing in this day that You and I cannot handle together. I praise You Lord and I give my day to You right now. I adore You and I am grateful to You for all the beautiful things that You are doing in my life and in my ministry. Daddy, You are in charge of my day so, I relax in Your presence knowing that all is well with me. Your glory has risen upon me and I am manifesting that glory today everywhere I go. Your power, beauty and excellence are revealed through me to my world as I walk worthy of You Lord unto all pleasing and as I display Your wonderful deeds and perfections. Lord, You have called me out of darkness unto glory and virtue. Therefore, I am sanctified from evil. There are no mishaps or destruction on my path. In my path are life, peace, victory and prosperity.

As I go out today, the land is subdued before me and I dwell in safety in it. The everlasting God is my place of safety and His hands will hold me up forever. As He promised me in **Deuteronomy 33:27**, He will force my enemies out ahead of me saying, *"Destroy the enemy."* Hallelujah! I am excellent and I do excellent things. God's plans for my life are coming to pass and I am exactly what somebody needs. God is leading me to the people He assigned me to. God's divine assignment is taking me places where I am celebrated and not tolerated. God is in me, He is with and for me; He is *"my shepherd and I shall not want. He makes me to lie down in green pastures; He leads me beside still waters. He restores my soul: He guides me in the paths of righteousness for his name's sake. Yea, though I walk through the valley of the shadow of death, I will fear no evil for thou art with me; Thy rod and thy staff, they comfort me. Thou prepares a table before me in the presence of mine enemies: Thou hast anointed my head with oil; My cup runs over. Surely Your goodness and loving kindness follow me all the days of my life; I am dwelling in the house of Jehovah forever"* **(Psalm 23).**

LORD, You are my light and my salvation; I fear no one. You protect me from all danger; I will never be afraid. Though a host should encamp against me, My heart shall not fear: Though war should rise against me, Even then will I be confident.

One thing have I asked of Jehovah, that will I seek after; That I may dwell in the house of Jehovah all the days of my life, To behold the beauty of Jehovah, And to inquire in his temple. For in the day of trouble he will keep me secretly in his pavilion: In the covert of his tabernacle will he hide me; He will lift me up upon a rock. And now shall my head be lifted up above mine enemies round about me. And I will offer in his tabernacle sacrifices of joy; I will sing, yea, I will sing praises unto Jehovah. (Psalms 23 and 27). These are my faith declarations and they are established unto me. The light of God's favor shines upon my ways. Hallelujah!

Day 25

I DECREE and AGREE that the Word of God is in my heart and in my mouth daily. It is prevailing against adverse circumstances and producing what it talks about in my spirit, soul and body. I know who I am and I am different; I am not the needy seeking help but the already favored of the Lord! I am marvelously helped and favored of the Lord! I am a matured child of God and I am not at the mercy of anyone. The Spirit of the Lord lives in me forever and all things are mine in Christ. Everything that I require for life and godliness is already granted me in Christ. I am blessed and I am a blessing in my world. I am living a life of power and favor. I am living in and through the power of the Holy Spirit and the Word daily, and I am working miracles in Jesus Name; Amen.

I know God can multiply my time and help me to get more done on a daily basis than I can do on my own. He can multiply my wisdom by giving me access to His wisdom when I ask Him because Jesus has been made wisdom unto me. I declare that He helps me make better decisions by His wisdom that is working in me. Just as He multiplied the five loaves and two fish, He can multiply whatever I bring before Him. God has new doors and gates of nations, in front of me that He is opening for me right now. My life is going from glory to glory; from grace to grace; from prosperity to prosperity; from faith to faith; and from success to success. God is working everything in my life for my advantage so; it is my set time to see more of God's faithfulness and goodness in my life and in my ministry. All this is because I have taken advantage of the finished work of my Lord Jesus Christ and I claim **Psalm 91**.

I boldly declare that I now dwell in the secret place of the Most High and I abide under the shadow of the Almighty. I say of You LORD, *"You are my refuge and my fortress: my God; in whom I trust."*

Surely You deliver me from the snare of the fowler and from the noisome pestilence. You cover me with Your feathers and under Your wings I trust: Your truth is my shield and buckler. Therefore, I am not afraid of the terror by night; nor of the arrow that flies by day; nor of the pestilence that walks in darkness; nor for the destruction that wastes at noonday. A thousand shall fall at my side and ten thousand at my right hand but they shall not come near me. Only with my eyes shall I behold and see the reward of the wicked. Because I have made the LORD which is my refuge; even the most High my habitation; there shall no evil befall me; neither shall any plague come near my dwelling. He has given his angels charge over me to keep me in all my ways.

They shall bear me up in their hands, lest I dash my foot against a stone. I shall tread upon the lion and adder: the Young lion and the dragon shall I trample under my feet. Because I have set my love upon the LORD, therefore will He deliver me: He has set me on high because I know His Name. These are my faith declarations and they are established unto me. The light of God's favor shines upon my ways. Hallelujah!

Day 26

I DECREE and AGREE that fear has no part in my life. For God did not give us a spirit of timidity, cowardice, craving, cringing and fawning fear, but He has given us a spirit of power, of love, of calm, of a well-balanced mind, of discipline and self-control. I am not ashamed of the Gospel of Jesus Christ nor am I afraid to proclaim it, for it is the power of God unto salvation. I preach and teach it in the power of the Holy Spirit. I know God's plan, desire and destiny for me is that I prosper in all I do and be in good health even as my soul prospers in Christ. He came to seek and to save the lost and I was lost. He found me and saved me. He gave me this ministry of telling others the Good News of the love of God for us in Christ; the Good News of spending a blissful eternity in the awesome presence of a loving Heavenly Father. He made what He did for me in Christ about two thousand years ago to become a legal and a vital reality in my life today. How can I keep quiet and not tell the untold of the love of God?

I rejoice in my salvation in Christ Jesus and I am eternally grateful to my Heavenly Father. Today, I know that God has given me His life –Zoe (eternal life). I now have His life and nature of righteousness. His Spirit lives in my spirit forever. God has put me in His class of beings and He has seated me with Christ Jesus in the Heavenly realms of glory and power. All my needs are supplied by God according to His riches in glory by Christ Jesus. When I call on the Name of Jesus, Heaven responds to me; because, the *LORD* says in **Psalm 91:14-16**:

> *"I will rescue those who love me. I will protect those who trust in my name. When they call on me, I will answer; I will be with them in trouble. I will rescue and honor them. I will reward them with long life and give them my salvation"* **(Psalm 91:14-16** *NLT).*

And also in **Psalm 34:1-11, I see my position and what I should continually do:**

> *"I will bless the LORD at all times: his praise shall continually be in my mouth. My soul shall make her boast in the LORD: the humble shall hear thereof, and be glad. O magnify the LORD with me, and let us exalt his name together. I sought the LORD, and he heard me, and delivered me from all my fears. They looked unto him, and were lightened: and their faces were not ashamed. This poor man cried, and the LORD heard him, and saved him out of all his troubles. The angel of the LORD encampeth round about them that fear him, and delivereth them. O taste and see that the LORD is good: blessed is the man that trusteth in him. O fear the LORD, ye his saints: for there is no want to them that fear him. The Young lions do lack, and suffer hunger: but they that seek the LORD shall not want any good thing. Come,*

ye children, hearken unto me: I will teach You the fear of the LORD"

These are my faith declarations and they have been made good by the High Priest of my professions; my Lord Jesus Christ who is my great High Priest. The light of God's favor shines upon my ways. Hallelujah!

Day 27

I DECREE and AGREE with God who said that His favor will last for a lifetime and that His goodness and mercy shall follow me all the days of my life. No matter what is going on in the world, I know that my Lord Jesus Christ brought me out of the world. Therefore, although I live in the world, I am no longer of the world. Armed with this knowledge, I use my energy to believe God's Word and God's Word prevails in my life and in my circumstances. It can only get better for me because my life is in God's hands. I am the righteousness of God in Christ Jesus and my steps are ordered of the Lord. I can neither fail, nor be defeated because I am in Him who has made me more than a conqueror. I have past conquering; I am now enjoying the glory that followed Jesus' sufferings on my behalf. I am on top, unstoppable and indestructible because I am in God and God is in me, for me and with me no matter who is against me.

I am on a divine assignment and no matter the opposition, I am a winner because God is for me; He fights my battles for me. Therefore, I am a victor because the Lord Jesus has already won the battle. He led captivity captive so the devil has no right to attack me anymore. I am born again to take possession of what belongs to me in Christ. My Lord Jesus by accomplishing His mission on planet earth, qualified me to live a life of purpose, peace, love, plenty, glory and fullness of joy. As a result of my new life in Christ, I am peculiar and strange to the world. I am backed by divinity and as a result, I am not controlled by the forces of this world system; the Greater One dwells in me. He loves me passionately and He is in charge of my life forever. I am the extension and representative of the risen Christ on earth and I have the life of God in me. I am enjoying the life that I carry in my spirit as well as my physical life; nothing can frustrate me. I am unique. I am God's best and there is power in my mouth.

When I call on the Name of Jesus, all the knees of Satan, his cohorts, sickness, disease, infirmities, poverty, lack and oppression of any kind bow and every tongue confesses that Jesus Christ is Lord to the glory of God the Father! I will never be broke another day in my life. I am in Christ; I was recreated in righteousness and true holiness. God gave birth to me in Christ and He gave me imaginative power; I am a matured son in the household of God. The Holy Spirit is my creative ability that is inside me. I diligently look into the mirror of God, the Bible; I see my image, the glory of God. I continually look into the Word of God and as a result, I am constantly been changed into that glory that I see in the mirror of God's Word. I see all that God has given me in Christ and I call them forth to become realities for me to enjoy here and now. This is the reality of my life in Christ! Glory be to God! I refuse to be religious. Religion is man's attempts to impress God. It is an attitude that says "I can make something of myself; I can earn God's favor." Although it may lead to works that are charitable, this attitude is fatally opposed to the grace of God. It causes man to stand when he should bow. My life is by His grace from start to finish. Amen. These are my faith declarations and they are established unto me. The light of God's favor shines upon my ways. Hallelujah!

Day 28

I DECREE, DECLARE and AGREE that I am equipped for every good work that God has planned for me. I am anointed and empowered by the Creator of the universe. Therefore, because of the finished work of Christ, every bondage and every limitation have been broken off of me and off of everyone associated with me. This is my time to shine and express His glory, power and righteousness through the Holy Spirit. I do not struggle to make things happen because I am the living tabernacle of divinity. I have the life of God in me because I have the Spirit of God in me. God is my life and He is my strength. He is my Heavenly Father and I have a loving intimate relationship with Him. My Lord Jesus Christ is my wisdom and my peace. God has empowered and exalted me; I create my world by His creative ability in me.

God has abundantly released His grace and His gift of righteousness to me and I have received and made them mine by the power of the Holy Spirit. I rule and reign in life through Jesus Christ my Lord. Today, God's grace is in abundance in my life and in my ministry. His blessings in my life and ministry are ever increasing because in Christ Jesus my Lord, He blessed me with all spiritual blessings in the heavenly places. I have the grace advantage; therefore I can never be disadvantaged. I am full of the anointing of the Holy Spirit and it is overflowing in my life. I am changing my world through this anointing. I have the competitive advantage; therefore, I am always a winner. I am winning my world with love and the Word of God, by the Holy Spirit.

God's Word is my agent for absolute change. The Word of God is building me and revealing to me who I am. The Word is eternal and tangible. It is uplifting me and putting me into new levels of success in my life and in my ministry. The Word has enlightened my life; so there is no more darkness in my life. God has called me into His light and made me His light. I have become the light of the world. The Lord Jesus is my Defense through His Spirit so, who can be against me and succeed? Nobody! And no weapon formed against me shall prosper.

God chose me; even when I did not know Him and I was in rebellion against Him. He had mercy on me and called me to live a glorious life of excellence in Christ. He chose me to be gracious to me and I am eternally grateful to You, Daddy! I am the best of God! God's dreams are coming to pass through me. God has deposited everything I will ever need inside me and although I do not yet see them physically, I believe God's Word. I call forth the things "that are not as if they were" and they become realities in my physical world. I am living by God's Kingdom principles and it can only get better for me in every area of my family life and in my ministry. My life is upwards and forwards only. I am a winner and a success all the time by His Spirit and by His Word. I know that God's Word works every time and everywhere so that I do not hesitate to speak it forth. Glory is to the Wonderful Name of Jesus my Lord. These are my faith declarations and they are established unto me. The light of His favor shines upon my path continually! Hallelujah!

Day 29

I DECREE, DECLARE and AGREE with God that nothing is impossible for me. Therefore, I boldly pray God size prayers and I expect God to show Himself strong and mighty on my behalf. God does great and amazing things through my life and I know that He has chosen me out of this world. He has separated me unto a life of purpose, victory and success. He has accepted me in the beloved and He is manifesting Himself to me and through me by His Spirit in Jesus' Name. Praise God that I am the chosen of the Lord! Father, in the Name of Jesus, I take dominion in my world, in my entire family and in my home. I rebuke lack of genuine faith in God. In Jesus' Name, I rebuke the evil spirits behind poverty, sickness, disease, and death of any type.

I declare salvation in Christ Jesus for everyone that comes into contact with me in my world, in my entire family and in my home. I declare that there is spiritual and physical life, health, wealth, peace, faith and joy in the lives of the people in my world, in my entire family and in my home. I declare that I am an excellent leader in God's Kingdom. Because the Greater One lives in me, I am confident, bold, considerate, kind, caring, determined, respectful to others, helpful, reliable, dependable, brave, careful, devoted and committed to God. Father, I know and I rejoice that You are the One who is the Source of my blessings and success. The arm of man fails most of the time; therefore, I do not need to resort to trying to win the favor of those that I consider significant people in my life.

Thank You Daddy, for it is Your favor upon me that sets me up for recognition, promotion, and increase. Hallelujah! Daddy, I thank You for making my path to be the path of the just which shines brighter and brighter unto the perfect day. By the power of Your Spirit and through Your Word, I make progress daily with giant strides. My life is the testimony of Your grace, mercy and provisions in my Lord Jesus Christ. Lord, I am what You say that I am and I can do what You say that I can do. I have what You say that I have and my faith in Your love for me is the evidence that all Your blessings concerning me in Your Word are now my present–hour possession. I am in the center of Your will for my life; where all things are synchronized and function to my advantage in Jesus' Name; Amen.

Lord, I am conscious of all You have made me and given me by Your finished work, and I am eternally grateful. I refuse to be sick because You have made me whole by Your stripes. I refuse to be broke because You made me rich by becoming poor so that through Your poverty, I might become rich and I am rich. I refuse to be under the dominion of sin because You who knew no sin was made sin so that I might be made the righteousness of God and I am the righteousness of God in You today. I thank You Lord for giving me such a beautiful life of dominion, power, and victory through Your finished work. I experience success and prosperity in all my affairs daily because I am in You and You are in me. My life is the manifestation of Your excellence, virtues and perfections. These are my declarations and they are established unto me. The light of God's favor shines upon my ways consistently. Hallelujah!

Day 30

I DECREE AND DECLARE that God is in control of my life; therefore, I have no room for worry. He can take what was meant for my harm and turn it around and use it for my advantage. I am governed by God's providence. God's wonderful plan is in effect in my life and in my ministry. I am growing by His plan and His plan is not to indulge me but to enlarge me. I am graced by His desires and I know that Jesus watches over me. His eyes are upon me and they go to and fro throughout the earth seeking on whose behalf to be strong —He is strong on my behalf! Jesus is my High Priest and He makes good my faith declarations. He knows me by name and *"He ever lives to make intercessions"* for me. According to **Hebrews 7:25**: He is able to save me to the uttermost because; I came to God by Him.

I am gladdened by His Presence and in His Presence is fullness of joy and pleasures forever more are at His Right Hand. I am guarded by His power. The will of God can never take me to where the grace of God cannot keep me. God has a plan and a destiny for me to fulfill and I am confident that I am on course in Christ. The Greater

One; my divine Counselor lives in me and He shepherds my life by leading me every step of the way. I am fulfilling my God-given destiny in Christ. Jesus is my "I AM" and He is eternally present in and with me. No matter what, I must always remember that the "I AM" is my God, that He loves me and that He knows me personally.

He is for me and nothing and no one can be against me and succeed. Jesus is "I AM" for me; what then is my need? I just fill in the gap. I am guided by His purpose and I am united with Him forever according to **Romans 8:28-39** (GNB):

> *"We know that in all things God works for good with those who love him, those whom he has called according to his purpose. Those whom God had already chosen he also set apart to become like his Son, so that the Son would be the first among many believers. And so those whom God set apart, he called; and those he called, he put right with himself, and he shared his glory with them. In view of all this, what can we say? If God is for us, who can be against us? Certainly not God, who did not even keep back his own Son, but offered him for us all! He gave us his Son—will he not also freely give us all things? Who will accuse God's chosen people? God himself declares them not guilty! Who, then, will condemn them? Not Christ Jesus, who died, or rather, who was raised to life and is at the right side of God, pleading with him for us!*
>
> *Who, then, can separate us from the love of Christ? Can trouble do it, or hardship or persecution or hunger or poverty or danger or death? As the scripture says: For Your sake we are in danger of death at all times; we are treated like sheep that are going to be slaughtered." No, in all these things we have complete victory through him who loved us!* ***For I am certain that nothing can separate us from his***

love: neither death nor life, neither angels nor other heavenly rulers or powers, neither the present nor the future, neither the world above nor the world below—**there is nothing in all creation that will ever be able to separate us from the love of God which is ours through Christ Jesus our Lord." This is the reality of my life in Christ.**

These are my faith declarations and they are established unto me. The light of God's favor shines upon my ways. Hallelujah!

Day 31

I know that I am still here in a fallen world but I am also very conscious that I do not belong here and that I belong to God's eternal Kingdom. I know that God is love and that He loves me completely because of the finished work of Christ Jesus my Lord. I am still here because God wants me to be here. Everything He does for me is rooted in His love for me. Therefore, I trust Him completely. Thank You Daddy!

In **John 17:11-26**, the Lord Jesus prayed the following prayer to the Father on my behalf and on the behalf of all who would believe in Him and heed His words. Today, I appropriate the blessings and the benefits of His prayer in my life and in the lives of everyone in my lineage and sphere of contact:

> "And now I am no more in the world, but these are in the world, and I come to thee. Holy Father, keep through thine own name those whom thou hast given me that they may be one, as we are. While I was with them in the world, I kept them in thy name: those that thou gavest me I have kept and none of them is lost, but the son of perdition; that the scripture might be fulfilled. And now come I to thee; and these things I speak in the world, that they might have my joy fulfilled in themselves. I have given them thy word; and the world hath hated them, because they are not

of the world, even as I am not of the world. I pray not that thou shouldest take them out of the world, but that thou shouldest keep them from the evil. They are not of the world, even as I am not of the world.

Sanctify them through thy truth: thy word is truth. As thou hast sent me into the world, even so have I also sent them into the world. And for their sakes I sanctify myself, that they also might be sanctified through the truth. Neither pray I for these alone, but for them also which shall believe on me through their word; That they all may be one; as thou, Father, art in me, and I in thee, that they also may be one in us: that the world may believe that thou hast sent me. And the glory which thou gavest me I have given them; that they may be one, even as we are one: I in them, and thou in me, that they may be made perfect in one; and that the world may know that thou hast sent me, and hast loved them, as thou hast loved me.

Father, I will that they also, whom thou hast given me, be with me where I am; that they may behold my glory, which thou hast given me: for thou lovedst me before the foundation of the world. O righteous Father, the world hath not known thee: but I have known thee, and these have known that thou hast sent me. And I have declared unto them thy name, and will declare it: that the love wherewith thou hast loved me may be in them, and I in them."

He tells me to study and meditate on His Word not as a daily chore, but as my source of spiritual nourishment and guidance. He loves me and wants me to have good success; all-round success. He loves me too much to let me live the life on earth that is outside of His plan and purpose for me in Christ Jesus. I can only have His kind of success when I study, meditate and live by His Word. Therefore, by the help of the Holy Spirit who reveals the Word of God to me and brings the presence of the Lord to me, I am determined to read, to study, to meditate and to live by the Word of God.

Therefore, I am above the circumstances of this world and I lack nothing good because the Lord is my Shepherd. I know that whatever may seem like a need in my life right now is already met in Christ by my loving and gracious Father God. I do not deserve anything but His grace has given me all things to enjoy; even here on earth. He makes all things beautiful in His time and according to His purpose. He is working His eternal purpose out in my life and I trust Him completely. He knows how and when to give me what I need to live godly in this life. He is never late. When He does it, is the right and best time. This is why I do not see any reason to fret, worry, and murmur or complain. There may be things I do not understand but I know my Heavenly Father has the complete picture and He is working all things out for my good. He called me according to His purpose and I love Him. In His timing and election, all the pieces of my life puzzle will beautifully fit together for His praise and glory. God's timing and choices are always the best and I patiently wait on Him. This is His counsel for me in Psalm 37:2-7:

> *Trust in the LORD, and do good; so shalt thou dwell in the land, and verily thou shalt be fed. Delight thyself also in the LORD; and he shall give thee the desires of thine heart. Commit thy way unto the LORD; trust also in him; and he shall bring it to pass. And he shall bring forth thy righteousness as the light, and thy judgment as the noonday. Rest in the LORD, and wait patiently for him: fret not thyself because of him who prospereth in his way, because of the man who bringeth wicked devices to pass.*

God's amazing plan for my life and my ministry is taking me places that I never dreamed I could be. Having received the abundance of grace and the gift of righteousness, I was born to rule and reign in life through Christ Jesus my Lord. This is my consciousness and the reality of God's Word concerning me. God said to me, *"Be still and know that I am God."* Therefore, I do not have a care in the world and I do not have anything to worry about. I am confident that God loves me and that I love Him. He is in complete control of my entire life forever. These are my faith declarations and they are established unto me. The light of God's favor shines upon my ways continually. Hallelujah!

WORK CITED WITH PERMISSION

At 10:37 pm on **April 25, 2013**, Jack Coley <jack@truthpressure.com> wrote:

"Pastor Mary,
*You can use what You wish on the site but everything is copyrighted. Just make a footnote in Your book: **"Used by permission from truth-pressure.com"** For legal purposes, You can use this e-mail for Your records to that effect.*
Thank you, and God Bless.
Jack and Wanda Coley"

At 12:17 pm on **Apr 25, 2013**, Mary Ehichioya <mehich1@yahoo.com> wrote:

*"Jack & Huayni, I write to seek your permission to use sections of some of your articles on the power of the spoken Word in a book I am writing; GOD'S WORD WORKS (now titled, **THE WORD OF GOD IS WORKING:** EVERYTIME AND EVERYWHERE). Thank you and God bless you.*
Pastor Mary Ehichioya"